CHOP CHOP

THE KIDS' GUIDE TO COOKING REAL FOOD WITH YOUR FAMILY

Sally Sampson

Photographs by Carl Tremblay

Simon & Schuster Paperbacks

New York   London   Toronto   Sydney   New Delhi

Simon & Schuster Paperbacks
1230 Avenue of the Americas
New York, NY 10020

First Simon & Schuster trade paperback edition August 2013

SIMON & SCHUSTER PAPERBACKS and colophon are registered trademarks of
Simon & Schuster, Inc.

For information about special discounts for bulk purchases, please contact Simon & Schuster
Special Sales at 1-866-506-1949 or business@simonandschuster.com.

The Simon & Schuster Speakers Bureau can bring authors to your live event. For more
information or to book an event contact the Simon & Schuster Speakers Bureau at
1-866-248-3049 or visit our website at www.simonspeakers.com.

Designed by Vic DeRobertis
Photographs © Carl Tremblay
Food stylist: Catrine Kelty

Manufactured in the United States of America

10 9 8 7 6 5 4 3 2 1

Library of Congress Cataloging-in-Publication Data
Sampson, Sally
  ChopChop : the kids' guide to cooking real food with your family / Sally Sampson ;
photographs by Carl Tremblay.
    pages cm
    1. Cooking—Juvenile literature. 2. Cooking, American—Juvenile literature. I. Tremblay, Carl.
II. Title. III. Title : Chop chop.
  TX652.5.S27 2013
  647.5973—dc23   2013019616

ISBN 978-1-4516-8587-9
ISBN 978-1-4516-8589-3 (ebook)

For Ben and Lauren, who taught me everything
there is to know about family

—S.S.

Contents

DINNER

DESSERT

DRINKS

Kids! Start Here!

You are going to love cooking. Maybe you already do, and that's why someone got you this cookbook—or maybe you've been thinking it would be great to start, and you've never picked up a spatula in your life (in that case: a spatula is a thing you use to flip food as it's cooking—more on that later). Either way, this cookbook is a great place to start. The recipes we've collected here are designed to teach you basic cooking skills and to develop a set of good meals you'll know how to make—and that you'll be able to improvise from as you learn more. We know you don't need chicken fingers and buttered spaghetti at every meal, even though restaurant menus act like you do. But then again, you're probably not really going to get too excited about cooking a kale-and-grain casserole. So this book is in the middle—healthy basics that are delicious and good for you, and that teach you the skills you need to keep on cooking.

Like algebra, history, and the other things you're learning, cooking skills build on themselves: once you get a solid foundation, the rest becomes easier. So, if you can roast a chicken, you can make a chicken-salad sandwich and chicken soup—and we'll show you how. But try thinking of the kitchen as a lab: cooking is really just one big, tasty experiment. Sometimes it's going to go great, and you'll end up with an awesome meal. Sometimes it's going to go less great, and maybe you'll burn an egg or you'll make a pot of soup that everyone has to smile politely about because really it didn't turn out well. But mostly you're going to need to do a lot of tinkering, and you'll be like a mad scientist with the salt and the lemon, the cumin and the mint. And that's the key, really—to have the courage to try, on the one hand, and the patience to learn what makes food taste good, on the other. And also to consider some basic principles about what you're doing in the kitchen and why.

Basic Tips

Do it. Don't wait for someone to suggest that you cook. Get an adult's permission, and then get started: make a single snack recipe; pick a night that you'll make dinner with a parent every week; start packing your own lunch; volunteer to make breakfast on the weekend; invite a friend over to cook for or cook with. Your family and friends will be grateful, and you'll feel great.

Get inspired. Look through this book and use sticky notes to mark recipes that make your mouth water. Or do it in reverse: go to the supermarket or farmers' market, find the freshest, most appealing ingredients, and then pick a recipe that uses them.

Open your mind. There might be ingredients or flavors in here that you think you don't like, but we always encourage you to open your mind and try again. People change. You might have outgrown your old taste buds, and even though green olives used to seem too strong you might love them now. Or maybe you just had an idea about the way something would taste, but you never actually tried it. Either way, it's a really good habit to expand your horizons.

Use all your senses. Cooking requires you to look, listen, touch, smell, and taste—all the time. Let's say you're sautéing onions in a pan: you'll know they're getting done when they start to get clear and golden; you'll want to hear them sizzling gently but not crackling furiously; you'll feel them growing softer under the spatula as they cook; you'll smell them cooking and, if you cook them too long, you'll smell them burning; and you'll taste them to see when they've gotten sweet and perfect.

Taste. And taste again. Even though we've tested and retested all these really good recipes, following a recipe isn't enough—you'll need to taste dishes as they're cooking to see if they need more of anything to really make the flavor pop. More herbs? Another squeeze of lemon or a teensy bit of pepper? What matters is what *you* like.

More Basic Tips

Read through the whole recipe before you start. You want to make sure you have all the ingredients, and you also don't want to get to a step that surprises you or requires help that's not available.

Plan ahead. Figure out when you want it to be done, then look at the total time required for the recipe and work backward. It might take less time, if you have help, or longer, if you're brand-new to cooking and are working on your own.

Don't worry. If a recipe calls for "milk" or "mustard," it doesn't matter what kind you use. Use whatever your family likes. When we think it matters, we'll let you know.

Take your time. This is another good reason to plan ahead: you never want to rush. It's not safe, and it's not even fun. It's better for dinner to be a half an hour later than you planned than for you to hurry.

Pay attention. Don't look out the window while you're chopping onions; keep your eyes on a sizzling pan; reread the recipe as you go so that you don't forget any steps or ingredients. (Although you inevitably will forget something at some point, and that's part of the process, too!)

Clean up. That's pretty basic advice, but it's important—your family is going to offer you way more encouragement (and thanks) if there's not a kitchen full of dirty pots and pans after every cooking experiment you try. It's often customary for the people who didn't cook to do the dishes, and that's fine, too! (And something to remember when someone else cooks.)

Write in this book. Make notes about what you've liked (or not liked), what changes you've made or would want to make next time, and what substitutions you think could work for ingredients that are preferable or in season. If you don't want to write right on the recipes, use sticky notes.

Wash Your Hands Before You Start

Give them a good scrub before you do any cooking or after you touch raw meat or egg. If you are wearing jewelry, take it off.

1. Wet your hands with warm water.
2. Add soap and rub your hands together.
3. Scrub the back of your hands, palms, fingers, between your fingers, under your nails.
4. Keep going while you sing all the way through "Happy Birthday."
5. Rinse well.
6. Dry your hands with a clean towel or paper towel.

Parents! Start Here!

What makes a healthy family? It's not an easy question, but the cookbook you're holding in your hands right now is going to help answer it. Learning to cook is a wonderful—and wonderfully healthy—thing for your kids to do. Whether it's about nurturing their bodies with healthy food, nurturing relationships at the dinner table, or nurturing happiness through new skills and accomplishments, cooking has so much to offer children. Kids who cook cultivate both pride in themselves and a lifetime of healthy habits in their families. You won't need to bug these children about what they should be eating—once they learn how to make good, wholesome food, then that's what they'll like to eat. And it's effortless, in a way—you focus on the fun, and the rest follows naturally.

Also, not to state the obvious, but kids who learn to cook will make you dinner. Considering the crazy juggling act that so many of us are living, and the difficulty of getting meals on the table, this is no small thing! And cooking means being part of the solution (rather than part of the hungry mob), which is something your kids will feel good about. It's also just enjoyable to cook with kids: it's a low-key way to spend time together, to share your family's values around food and eating, and to talk about things that have nothing at all to do with cooking (haven't you found that kids will often share the most in a side-by-side activity, rather than in a deliberate conversation?). For children and grown-ups alike, making a meal is an act of devotion, of generosity: you commit your time and energy to putting a meal on the table for the people you love. What could be better? Plus, kids soak up new ideas like sponges, so there's no better time than now for them to pick up kitchen skills—in addition to all the literacy, math, chemistry, logic, and problem solving they'll take in along the way.

Speaking of sponges . . . having kids in the kitchen can be kind of messy at first and that can be frustrating. But if you keep plenty of rags and paper towels on hand, your kids can learn to clean up after themselves, as part of the whole process. Think of it as an investment: at first it's actually harder to get dinner on the table with the kids helping—and then, over time, it gets much, much easier.

But this cookbook isn't really a political rallying cry, an educational treatise, or a manifesto about good health. It is above all friendly, engaging, aspirational, and inspirational. It's a book to be read from cover to cover on the couch or one recipe at a time in the kitchen; it should get bent and loved and splattered with salsa.

Essential Ingredients

One of the most important things to do if you want to become a good—and easygoing—cook is to have lots of ingredients in your pantry, refrigerator, and freezer. If you're well stocked with these essential ingredients, trips to the grocery store will be easier and take less time. Here's a list that makes sense for *ChopChop* recipes, but if there are ingredients your family doesn't like, feel free to skip them. If we've forgotten anything that you consider essential, be sure to add it to the list.

Pantry
Beans: black, dark red, white
Tomatoes, diced
Chicken broth
Canned tuna

Dry goods
All-purpose flour
Whole-wheat or white whole-
wheat flour
Kosher salt

In bottles and jars
Oils: olive and canola
Vinegar
Mustard

In the fridge
Eggs, large
Plain yogurt
Carrots
Celery
Lemons

In the pantry
Garlic
Onions

Not All Salt Is the Same
We like kosher salt for cooking everything, even desserts. Instead of plain salt-shaker salt (table salt), we'd like you to try kosher salt. Kosher salt is used by most chefs and for good reason: it brings out the flavor of food without making it taste salty. However, if you don't have it (or don't want to buy it), use what you have on hand.

Measurements
3 teaspoons = 1 tablespoon
4 tablespoons = ¼ cup
5 tablespoons plus 1 teaspoon = ⅓ cup
8 tablespoons = ½ cup
2 cups = 1 pint
4 cups = 1 quart
4 quarts = 1 gallon

Essential Equipment

It's not important to have a lot of fancy cooking equipment, but it is important to have some basics. Here's what we think you really need to have, but if you have, for instance, an 8-inch skillet, don't worry about getting a 10-inch.

Cutting board
Large skillet (10-inch)
Set of glass, ceramic, or stainless-steel
  mixing bowls
Measuring spoons
Measuring cup
Sharp knife (adult needed)
Spatulas (metal or rubber)
Vegetable peeler
Box grater (adult needed)
Medium-sized pot, with lid
Wooden spoon
Can opener

Colander or strainer
Pot holders
Clean dish towels

Good to have but not essential:
Blender (adult needed)
Whisk
Tongs
Rimmed baking sheet
Ladle (if you like to make soup)
Salad spinner (if you like to make salads)
Food processor (adult needed)
Clean kitchen scissors (adult needed)

Seasoning Experiment

One of the most important skills you can develop as a cook is learning to taste food. That means that you taste a dish before you serve it, to figure out if it needs anything—even if you've already added all the ingredients listed in the recipe! You have your own preferences and different ingredients will require different adjustments. You'll want to learn how to season food so that it tastes as good to you as it could possibly taste. To learn a little bit about some of the main seasoning elements, try this:

KITCHEN GEAR
Vegetable peeler

Sharp knife (adult needed)

Medium-sized pot, with lid

Colander

INGREDIENTS
1 potato, scrubbed or peeled, and cubed

1 lemon, cut in half

Kosher salt

Black pepper

Other seasonings, including salsa, ground cinnamon, pesto, any kind of vinegar, cayenne pepper, curry powder, fresh garlic, hot sauce, grated lemon zest and/or whatever else you like

INSTRUCTIONS
1. Put the potato in the pot, fill the pot halfway with cold water, and put it on the stove. Turn the heat to high and bring the pot to a boil (you'll know the water is boiling when you see bubbles breaking all over the surface).

2. Lower the heat to medium and cook until the potato is tender, about 15 minutes.

3. Put the colander in the sink. Pour the potatoes into the colander and set them aside until cooled, about 20 minutes.

Take a cube of potato and eat it plain. What does it taste like?

Sprinkle a little **salt** on a cube and taste it.

Squeeze a little **lemon juice** on a cube and taste it.

Grind or shake a little **pepper** on a cube and taste it.

Now **combine the seasonings** and figure out what your perfect balance is: How much salt? How much lemon? How much pepper? Is there one you prefer not to use?

Breakfast

Everyone says that breakfast is the most important meal of the day.

Well, it's true, so we're going to start this book by teaching you how to make a really good one.

Breakfast is important because it fills your "empty tank." It refuels your body and gets you going after a long night without food. It helps boost energy so you'll feel good, gives you some of the nutrients you need to be healthy, and even enables you to do better in school. That's not just us grown-ups talking: scientific studies prove that eating in the morning boosts brain power. So don't miss breakfast: Be sure to eat something good in the morning!

We know what school-day mornings are like: there's your comfy bed to get out of, teeth to be brushed, and backpacks to be packed. And the adults in your house are probably rushing around, too. So we're going to give you a few ideas for really quick breakfasts, ones that don't involve any cooking at all. But we're also going to give you some recipes that require either a little more time, for mornings that aren't rushed (try to make room for some of those), or a lot more time, for nice, slow weekends.

No-Cook Breakfasts

Cold cereal. Please encourage your adults to buy cereal with plenty of good ingredients like grains, nuts, and dried fruit, and without added sugar (or without a lot of added sugar). These cereals are generally not those advertised on TV and, as a rule, don't have sugar in the first five ingredients. Add fresh fruit and milk and/or plain yogurt.

Whole-wheat toast or multigrain bagel. Don't just think about topping them with sweet things. Instead, spread on any of the following: peanut butter, almond butter, ricotta cheese, Greek yogurt, White-Bean Dip (page 39), Classic Hummus (page 41), even Guacamole (page 42).

Why eat whole-wheat or multigrain bread? They are both much healthier than white bread because they have more fiber, good oils, proteins, and vitamins. Bread becomes white because all the good stuff is taken out.

Plain yogurt. Instead of buying yogurt with the fruit already mixed in, add your own fresh fruit: bananas, fresh (or frozen) berries, apples (they're particularly good shredded), or pears. Add dried fruit, nuts, toasted wheat germ, or a sprinkle of Granola (page 10). You can even make a breakfast parfait by layering ingredients in a glass.

Cottage cheese or ricotta cheese. Add fresh or frozen berries, dried fruit, applesauce, nuts, or toasted wheat germ or wheat bran. Or spread some on a plain rice cake or a piece of whole-wheat toast.

Fruit. Cut up your favorite fruits into bite-sized pieces and make a salad, or thread them onto a skewer to make a colorful kabob. Or spread peanut butter or almond butter on an apple or a banana.

DID YOU KNOW?

Breakfast doesn't have to be sweet: In Israel, they eat salad for breakfast. In China, dumplings or *congee*, a rice soup, is a typical first meal of the day. In Cataluña, a region of Spain, they eat *pan con tomate*: bread rubbed with fresh tomato and drizzled with kosher salt and olive oil. French breakfast eaters sometimes start their day with crêpes or quiche, and Japanese kids might eat miso soup first thing in the morning. **Breakfast can even be spicy:** In Mexico, you might get off to a good start with *huevos rancheros*, which is eggs with salsa and beans.

Smoothies

Smoothies take almost no time at all, but if your mornings are super rushed, you can put everything in the blender the night before, put the top on tightly, and refrigerate. Then, when you wake up, put the blender on the base and whir away. Or, for another time saver, try measuring your solid ingredients into a plastic freezer bag; label it with the contents (such as "1 cup peaches and bananas, 1 tablespoon almonds") and the amount of liquid you'll need to add (such as "add 1 cup milk"), then freeze until you're ready for a smoothie.

Mix-and-Match Smoothie

ADULT NEEDED: YES · HANDS-ON TIME: 10 MINUTES · TOTAL TIME: 10 MINUTES · MAKES: 2 SERVINGS

Put a cool, fruity smoothie in your thermos, and if you don't drink it for breakfast, you'll be psyched for it at snack time or lunchtime. Just give it a shake before drinking, to make sure all the ingredients are blended.

There are certain fruits that are particularly good with other fruits, and with other ingredients, too. But don't take our word for it: experiment to your heart's delight! For example: one ChopChopper adds spinach to her smoothie because she doesn't think she gets enough vegetables (and surprisingly, it doesn't make the smoothie taste like spinach). Another ChopChopper adds almond butter because she loves how smooth and creamy it makes her smoothie. Plus it's a great way to add even more protein.

KITCHEN GEAR
Measuring cup
Measuring spoons
Sharp knife (adult needed)
Cutting board
Blender (adult needed)

INSTRUCTIONS
1. Put your liquid ingredient(s) in the blender, then add whatever cut-up fruit and the extras you choose.
2. Put the blender top on tightly. Turn the blender to medium and blend until the mixture is smooth, about 2 minutes.
3. Divide the smoothie between 2 glasses.
4. Serve right away, or cover and refrigerate up to 4 hours.

INGREDIENTS

FRUIT, FRESH OR FROZEN	+	LIQUID	+	EXTRAS	+	IF YOU LIKE
1 cup (mix and match)		1 cup		1–2 tablespoons		
peaches berries apples oranges banana pineapple mango		½ cup plain yogurt plus ½ cup water or low-fat or whole milk or soy milk, almond milk, flax milk or rice milk or coconut water		almonds, walnuts, or pecans or wheat germ or ground flaxseed or peanut or almond butter		1 cup kale or spinach or 2 ice cubes or ½ teaspoon cinnamon or vanilla or 1 teaspoon honey or real maple syrup

Try these combinations:

Eggnog Smoothie
1 cup plain yogurt
1 overripe banana, sliced

EXTRAS
1 tablespoon almonds
1 teaspoon honey or real maple syrup (if you like it sweet)
¼ teaspoon vanilla extract
1 pinch ground nutmeg
4 ice cubes

Strawberry Banana
1 cup plain yogurt
1 tablespoon frozen orange juice concentrate
3 tablespoons water
1 overripe banana, sliced
6 strawberries, hulled ("hulled" means with the green top and the stem removed)

EXTRAS
2 teaspoons honey

Tropical Smoothie
¾ cup plain yogurt
1 orange, peeled and chopped
½ cup overripe banana slices (frozen preferred)
½ cup fresh or frozen pineapple chunks
1 tablespoon shredded unsweetened coconut

EXTRAS
2 ice cubes
1 tablespoon almond or peanut butter

Green Monster Smoothie
1 cup plain yogurt
½ cup orange juice
2 cups chopped kale (discard the thick middle rib before chopping) or spinach
1 overripe banana, sliced
1 apple, scrubbed, cored and chopped
1 cup frozen blueberries

EXTRAS
2 tablespoons almonds or walnuts, toasted

Frozen Banana How-To

To help make any smoothie thicker, have frozen banana slices ready to go. Just peel an overripe banana and slice it into thin rounds with a butter knife. (You know it's overripe when it has a lot of brown spots and is soft to the touch. The inside becomes really mushy and sweet, which is perfect for smoothies.) Put the slices in a resealable plastic bag and freeze.

Oatmeal

Oatmeal makes a delicious breakfast that will keep you feeling full all morning. There are three kinds of oats: steel-cut, old-fashioned, and instant oats. Each is good for you as long as they don't have added sugar or artificial ingredients (so stay away from those little packets). Our recipe (below) uses steel-cut oats. They take longer than the others, but their nutty taste and chewy texture make them well worth the wait. Even though it's more work, many people never go back to the faster version once they've tried steel-cut.

Hearty Steel-Cut Oatmeal

Although cooking steel-cut oats takes much longer than old-fashioned oats, the taste is so much better we're sure you'll think it's worth the wait. Plus, once you get used to organizing yourself to cook oatmeal this way, you won't miss the old mushy oatmeal!

ADULT NEEDED: YES • HANDS-ON TIME: 5 MINUTES • TOTAL TIME: 35 MINUTES • MAKES: 2 SERVINGS

KITCHEN GEAR
Measuring cup
Small pot
Pot holder
Large spoon

INGREDIENTS
½ cup steel-cut oats
2 cups cold tap water

INSTRUCTIONS
1. Put the oats and water in the pan and put the pan on the stove. Turn the heat to high and bring to a boil.
2. As soon as it boils, lower the heat to very low and cook until the oatmeal is tender (soft, but not soggy) and the water has been absorbed, 25 to 30 minutes.
3. Serve right away with any of the toppings listed above.

Top This
Add any or all of these to each serving:
2 tablespoons low-fat milk or yogurt
2 tablespoons chopped apples or pears, or fresh berries
¼ banana, sliced, diced, or mashed
1 tablespoon raisins, dried cranberries, dates, or chopped apricots
1 tablespoon toasted chopped walnuts, pecans, or almonds
1 teaspoon flaxseed or toasted wheat germ, wheat bran, or oat bran
1 teaspoon real maple syrup, honey, or brown sugar, or ½ to ⅔ teaspoon agave syrup

DID YOU KNOW?

Agave syrup, also called agave nectar, is a liquid sweetener that comes from the agave plant that grows in Mexico and South Africa. If you use agave, start with a small amount: it's even sweeter than sugar and honey.

Overnight Oatmeal

If your mornings are rushed and the last recipe takes too much time, just put in 10 minutes of prep time the night before and your steel-cut oats will be almost instant!

ADULT NEEDED: YES • HANDS-ON TIME: 20 MINUTES (THE NIGHT BEFORE) AND 10 MINUTES IN THE MORNING
TOTAL TIME: 30 MINUTES, PLUS OVERNIGHT • MAKES: 2 SERVINGS

KITCHEN GEAR
Measuring cup
Small pot
Pot holder
Large spoon

INGREDIENTS
½ cup steel-cut oats
2 cups cold tap water

INSTRUCTIONS

The night before:
1. Put the oats and water in the small pot and put it on the stove.
2. Turn the heat to high and bring to a boil. As soon as it boils, turn the heat off.
3. Let sit until it cools to room temperature, about 20 minutes.
4. Cover and refrigerate at least overnight and up to 2 days.

In the morning:
1. Remove the cover.
2. Put the pot on the stove and turn the heat to high. Bring to a boil.
3. As soon as it boils, lower the heat to very low and cook, stirring occasionally, until the oatmeal is tender and the water has been absorbed, about 5 minutes.
4. Add whatever toppings you like (see page 7) and serve right away.

DID YOU KNOW?

Oats are actually seeds (grain) that grow in clusters at the end of a long stalk of grass. Harvested oats have a hard outer husk that you can't eat. When the husk is removed and the seeds are toasted, they're called "groats," which is a great word, right? By the time they get to your breakfast table, they're labeled either steel-cut, rolled, or instant. What's the difference? Steel-cut oats are sliced two or three times to make smaller chunks. Rolled oats are steamed, then rolled flat and dried. Rolled oats cook faster, but steel-cut oats are nuttier and chewier. Instant oats are chopped-up rolled oats that cook quickly.

Oatmeal, like other grains, can be soaked overnight for faster cooking the next morning. Heat travels through the grains much faster than water does and soaking gives the water a head start (you can actually see the water's effect because the oats get thicker). In the end, soaking will lead to faster cooking the next morning because the water will already have gone through the grains.

Homemade Instant Oatmeal

Skip store-bought instant oatmeal, and make your own by grinding up regular oats! It's healthier, less expensive, and just as quick—thanks to our do-ahead method that lets you prepare a lot at once, and then make breakfast one bowl at a time.

ADULT NEEDED: YES • HANDS-ON TIME: 10 MINUTES • TOTAL TIME: 10 MINUTES • MAKES: 6 SERVINGS

KITCHEN GEAR
Measuring cup

Measuring spoons

Blender or food processor
(adult needed)

Airtight container ("Airtight" means that it closes really well and that even air can't get in or out.)

Heatproof bowl

Spoon

INGREDIENTS
3 cups old-fashioned oats

½ teaspoon kosher salt

INSTRUCTIONS

To make instant oatmeal:

1. Put 1 cup oats and the salt in the blender or food processor. Make sure the top is on tight, so you don't spray the powder all over the kitchen! Turn the blender to medium and blend until the oats are powdered.
2. Add the rest of the oats and put the top on tightly.
3. Turn the blender or food processor on and off (this is called "pulsing") until the oats are mostly broken down. You may need to stop and shake up the blender jar if the oat powder at the bottom is stopping the blade from moving.
4. Put the oat mixture in an airtight container or plastic bag and store up to 3 months.

For each serving:

½ cup oatmeal mixture

¾ cup boiling water (adult needed)

1. Put the oatmeal mixture in a heatproof bowl.
2. Pour the boiling water over it, stir, and let sit for 1 minute. Stir again, add whatever toppings (see page 7) you like, and serve right away.

SAFETY ⚠ TIP

Always be careful with blades, as well as knives: Remember to keep your fingers away from the sharp blades.

Why do you need an airtight container?
Airtight containers stop the flow of moisture, so that dry foods can stay dry and wet foods can stay wet. Many of the chemical reactions that cause food to decay, like the browning of apples or avocados, require oxygen, so without access to air these can't happen.

Oven Mitts vs. Pot Holders
Most oven mitts are too big for kids. Try them on before you hold anything hot to be sure they are safe for you. Pot holders may be a better and safer choice.

Granola

Granola uses a lot of different ingredients, but you can also change them as you like: substitute pecans for the walnuts, currants for the raisins, or dates for the apricots. Granola is great to serve with milk, on top of yogurt or cottage cheese, even mixed into cookie dough. If you don't have two baking sheets, either halve the recipe or bake half at a time.

ADULT NEEDED: YES • HANDS-ON TIME: 20 MINUTES • TOTAL TIME: 45 MINUTES • MAKES: 14–15 CUPS

KITCHEN GEAR
2 large baking sheets with sides
Large bowl
Small bowl
Measuring cup
Measuring spoons
Large spoon
Large airtight container
Pot holder

INGREDIENTS
4 cups old-fashioned oats
1 cup wheat germ
1 cup ground flaxseed
1 cup unsweetened coconut
1 cup raw sunflower seeds
1 cup sliced or chopped raw almonds
1 cup chopped raw walnuts
1 cup raw pumpkin seeds
½ cup sesame seeds
1 teaspoon kosher salt
1 cup unsalted butter, melted, or canola or olive oil
¾ cup honey or real maple syrup
2 teaspoons vanilla extract
1 cup raisins (any color is fine)
1 cup dried cranberries
1 cup diced dried apricots

INSTRUCTIONS
1. Turn the oven on and set it to 300 degrees. Using your clean hand or a paper towel, lightly coat the baking sheets with canola or olive oil.
2. Put the oats, wheat germ, flaxseed, coconut, sunflower seeds, almonds, walnuts, pumpkin seeds, sesame seeds, and salt in the large bowl and mix well.
3. Put the butter or oil, honey or real maple syrup, and vanilla extract in the small bowl and mix well. Add the butter mixture to the oat mixture and stir until the butter is completely worked through the mix.
4. Put half the mixture on each baking sheet and press evenly and firmly around the sheet. Put the sheets in the oven and bake until crisp and golden, about 15 minutes.
5. Carefully take the baking sheets out of the oven with the potholder and put on top of the stove. The mixture should form into pieces, which you should break up and turn over. If it doesn't, just mix it.
6. Return the baking sheets to the oven until the other side is golden, 5 to 10 minutes.
7. Remove the sheets from the oven and set them on the stovetop.
8. When it has cooled completely, move the mixture to the large bowl. Add the raisins, cranberries, and apricots and mix well. Store in the airtight container.

Muesli

Muesli (*muse*-lee) is a traditional Swiss breakfast developed by Dr. Maximilian Oskar Bircher-Benner. It's made from uncooked oats, fruit, and, often, nuts. Although it sounds like a strange dish, muesli has a fresh-tasting chewiness (from the soaked oats), making it a nice change of pace from cooked oatmeal. *By Catherine Newman*

ADULT NEEDED: YES • HANDS-ON TIME: 5 MINUTES • TOTAL TIME: 10 MINUTES • MAKES: 2 SERVINGS

KITCHEN GEAR
Measuring cup
Box grater (adult needed)
2 cereal bowls

INGREDIENTS
1 cup old-fashioned oats
2 cups low-fat or whole milk
1 apple, scrubbed or peeled and grated on the large holes of a box grater

INSTRUCTIONS
1. Divide the oats between the 2 bowls. Pour half the milk in each bowl and let sit for 5 minutes.
2. Divide the shredded apple between the 2 bowls, stir, add any of the oatmeal toppings (see page 7), and eat right away.

Buttermilk Pancakes

Who doesn't love buttermilk pancakes? Ours are light and fluffy, with a little added texture from the cornmeal. If you have a hard time pouring the batter onto the skillet, try pouring it into a clean, empty squeeze bottle; it's really easy to squeeze out nice, even pancakes that way, and you can even spell your name on the pan or the griddle!

ADULT NEEDED: YES · HANDS-ON TIME: 10 MINUTES · TOTAL TIME: 20 MINUTES · MAKES: 8–12 SIX- TO EIGHT-INCH PANCAKES

KITCHEN GEAR
Large bowl
Fork or whisk
Measuring spoons
Small bowl
Large skillet
Ladle
Heatproof spatula

INGREDIENTS
1¾ cups all-purpose flour, or a combination of all-purpose flour and whole-wheat flour
¼ cup yellow cornmeal
1 teaspoon baking soda
2 teaspoons baking powder
¼ teaspoon kosher salt
2 cups buttermilk
½ cup low-fat or whole milk
2 large eggs
2 tablespoons canola or vegetable oil
Real maple syrup

INSTRUCTIONS
1. Put the flour, cornmeal, baking soda, baking powder, and salt in the large bowl and stir until it is combined.
2. Put the buttermilk, milk, eggs, and 1 tablespoon oil in the small bowl and stir to combine. Add the wet ingredients to the dry ingredients and mix until just combined. Do not keep mixing until it is smooth; you want it to be a little lumpy and bumpy. (You can cover and refrigerate batter up to 2 days.)
3. Put the skillet on the stove and turn the heat to medium. When it is hot, add the remaining 1 tablespoon oil.
4. Drop ladlefuls of batter into the skillet and cook until there are many little bubbles on the pancake's surface. Using the spatula, flip the pancakes over and cook until golden, about 2 minutes. Serve right away with real maple syrup.

Fancy That!
Pancake batter can be laced with different ingredients! Some of our favorites are blueberries, banana slices, chopped nuts, dried coconut, raspberries, and sliced strawberries.

DID YOU KNOW?

Real maple syrup is better than corn-syrup–based "pancake syrup." Think of real maple syrup as "concentrated tree juice": because it's made from the sap of maple trees, it's full of minerals that your body needs, including manganese and zinc. (Of course, it's still a kind of sugar, so don't get carried away.)

Why is it important to mix the batter so briefly? Mixing the batter produces stretchy protein molecules, called gluten. We don't want much of this to happen to the pancakes—it will make them tough instead of tender.

Don't have buttermilk? Instead of 2 cups buttermilk plus ½ cup milk use 2⅓ cups milk plus 1 tablespoon white vinegar.

DID YOU KNOW?

A German pancake is just a big baked bubble: Inside the oven, liquid from the batter turns to steam, which gets trapped within stretchy protein molecules in the flour, called gluten. When the pancake cools, the air bubbles cool and the steam turns back into water, which causes it to collapse.

German Pancake

Like a giant popover, this pancake turns puffy and delicious in the oven—an edible bowl for whatever fruit you want to fill it with! The key to success here is making sure the oven and the pan are really hot before you put the batter in.

ADULT NEEDED: YES • HANDS-ON TIME: 10 MINUTES • TOTAL TIME: 35 MINUTES • MAKES: 4–6 SERVINGS

KITCHEN GEAR
10-inch ovenproof skillet
Large bowl
Fork or whisk
Measuring spoons
Measuring cup
Pot holder
Sharp knife (adult needed)

INGREDIENTS
For the pancake:
1 tablespoon unsalted butter
4 large eggs
1 cup low-fat or whole milk
½ teaspoon vanilla extract
1 cup all-purpose flour
¼ teaspoon kosher salt

INSTRUCTIONS
1. Turn the oven on and set it to 450 degrees. Put the butter in the skillet, and put the skillet in the oven while you prepare the batter.
2. Put the eggs in the large bowl and, using the fork or whisk, stir until light and frothy. Add the milk and vanilla extract to the bowl and mix well. Add the flour and salt and stir until smooth.
3. When the oven is hot, use the pot holder to remove the skillet from the oven (ask your adult to do this, especially if you are using a heavy skillet).
4. Pour the batter into the hot skillet and carefully put it back in the oven.
5. Bake until very puffy and golden-brown around the edges, around 15 minutes. Remove the skillet from the oven and set it on the stovetop to cool for 1 minute—and watch the pancake deflate!
6. Cut into wedges, and serve right away.

Top This
Serve with confectioners' sugar, real maple syrup, Best-Ever Applesauce (page 143), or sliced bananas and strawberries.

French Toast

Try using different kinds of bread (multigrain, cinnamon raisin, anadama, even croissants), but be sure they are at least one day old. If the bread is too fresh, it won't absorb the egg mixture and your French toast will be soggy.

ADULT NEEDED: YES • HANDS-ON TIME: 25 MINUTES • TOTAL TIME: 25 MINUTES • MAKES: 4 SERVINGS

KITCHEN GEAR
Measuring cup
Measuring spoons
Fork or whisk
Large mixing bowl
Large skillet
Heatproof spatula

INGREDIENTS
¾ cup low-fat or whole milk
2 large eggs
¼ teaspoon vanilla extract
⅛ teaspoon ground cinnamon
2–3 tablespoons canola or vegetable oil
6 slices whole-wheat, oatmeal, or cinnamon raisin bread, 1 day old or more
Real maple syrup

INSTRUCTIONS
1. Put the milk, eggs, vanilla extract, and cinnamon in the large mixing bowl and stir until just combined.
2. Put the skillet on the stove and turn the heat to medium. When it is hot, carefully add the oil.
3. Dip the bread, 1 slice at a time, in the egg mixture and let sit until both sides are well coated with egg, about 30 seconds. If there is too much egg mixture on the bread, let it drip off before you cook it.
4. Put the bread on the hot skillet and cook until golden brown, about 3 minutes per side. Repeat with all the bread. Serve right away with real maple syrup.

Eggs

An egg is a perfect meal in a shell! Eggs are delicious, inexpensive, satisfying, and full of fantastic nutrients like protein and B vitamins. Plus, if you can cook an egg, you can make a meal—and not just breakfast, either: hard-cooked eggs or egg salad makes a great lunch, or you can fry up a couple of eggs for dinner and serve them with whole-wheat toast and fruit salad. When it comes to meals, there aren't rules you have to follow: If it's balanced and healthy—and you like it!—that sounds pretty good to us.

Scrambled Eggs

Scrambled eggs are eaten in most cultures, households, and restaurants. Why? They are easy, quick, healthy, delicious, inexpensive, and pair well with many ingredients. There are as many techniques and preferences for scrambled eggs as there are people. While we all have opinions about what's the best method, it's really for you to say what's just right for you. If you don't move the eggs around in the pan a lot, you get scrambled eggs that are more like an omelet: big, almost dense pieces. If you move the eggs around and whisk constantly, they will be smaller, fluffier, and creamier. Try it both ways. Just add a green salad or a fruit salad, and you're all set.

ADULT NEEDED: YES • HANDS-ON TIME: 10 MINUTES • TOTAL TIME: 10 MINUTES • MAKES: 1–2 SERVINGS

KITCHEN GEAR
Small bowl
Fork
Small skillet
Measuring spoons
Heatproof spatula

INGREDIENTS
2 large eggs
A pinch kosher salt
2 teaspoons olive, canola, or vegetable oil

INSTRUCTIONS
1. Crack the eggs, one at a time—at the midpoint between the more-rounded (wide) end and the pointier end of the egg—by hitting it quickly against the sharp edge of the bowl.

2. Hold the egg over the bowl with the cracked part facing up. Pry the shell open gently and allow the egg to slide into the bowl. Add a pinch of salt and, using the fork, beat until it is pale yellow.

3. Put the pan on the stove and turn the heat to medium. Add the oil and, when it is hot, carefully pour in the egg mixture.

4. The egg on the bottom of the pan, closest to the heat, will set first: drag the spatula across the bottom of the pan so that the egg that hasn't set yet can run underneath the egg that has. Keep pulling the cooked egg aside until all the runny egg has had a chance to cook. Serve right away, with toast, if you like.

How can you tell if an egg is fresh? Fill a bowl with cold tap water. Gently drop in a raw egg (still in the shell!): If it sinks, it's fresh, but if it floats, throw it away.

Top This
You can scramble vegetables into eggs as they're cooking! One way to do it is to cook the vegetables gently in the oil first, and then, when they're tender, add the eggs and scramble them together. Try:

- Sliced onion or scallions, greens and whites
- Sliced mushrooms
- Diced bell peppers or zucchini

And then there are ingredients that don't need to cook first. You can add these when you add the eggs:

- Diced tomatoes
- Shredded cheddar or crumbled feta cheese
- Diced baked tofu
- Chopped fresh herbs, like basil, dill, or parsley
- Baby spinach

Fried Eggs

Fried eggs are totally classic! Be sure to crack the egg into a glass cup first; it's safer, and you'll be less likely to bust the yolk if you use the glass to gently slide the egg into the hot skillet. Serve with toast or an English muffin, if you like.

ADULT NEEDED: YES • HANDS-ON TIME: 10 MINUTES • TOTAL TIME: 10 MINUTES • MAKES: 1–2 SERVINGS

KITCHEN GEAR
Small glass or cup
Small skillet
Measuring spoons
Heatproof spatula

INGREDIENTS
2 large eggs
½ teaspoon olive, canola, or
   vegetable oil
A pinch kosher salt

INSTRUCTIONS
1. Crack the eggs, one at a time, at the midpoint between the more-rounded (wide) end and the pointier end of the egg—by hitting it quickly against the sharp edge of the glass.
2. Hold the egg over the glass with the cracked part facing up. Pry the shell open gently and allow the egg to slide into the cup. Throw away the shell.
3. Put the skillet on the stove and turn the heat to medium. Let it heat up and after about 2 minutes, add the oil.
4. Slowly slide the egg from the glass to one side of the skillet. Repeat with the other egg right away.
5. When the eggs start to set, sprinkle with the salt. When the edges are solid, use the spatula to flip them over.
6. Cook until the yolks are cooked to your liking, about 1 minute. Serve right away.

Be Creative

Green Eggs No Ham: Make a fried-egg sandwich and top it with a few leaves of spinach and/or a slice of cheese.

Huevos Rancheros: Skip the toast and lay your fried egg on ½ cup warm, cooked pinto or black beans. Top with sliced avocado or a dollop of Guacamole (page 42), salsa, and a spoonful of plain yogurt, and serve with corn tortillas.

Frittata

A frittata is a great do-ahead breakfast. It's a cross between an omelet and a quiche. You can eat it hot or cold, alone or sandwiched between two slices of whole-grain bread. Plus, the protein in those eggs provides you with lots of energy for your day! We're giving you a basic recipe for making a veggie frittata, but check out the variations below for ideas on how to customize it.

ADULT NEEDED: YES • HANDS-ON TIME: 30 MINUTES • TOTAL TIME: 1 HOUR • MAKES: 4 SERVINGS

KITCHEN GEAR
Measuring spoons
Large ovenproof skillet
Cutting board
Sharp knife (adult needed)
Measuring cup
Large mixing bowl
Fork or whisk
Heatproof spatula or large spoon
Pot holders

INGREDIENTS
3 teaspoons olive, canola, or vegetable oil
1 onion, chopped
½ head broccoli or cauliflower
½ cup leftover cooked potatoes or cooked rice or day-old bread cubes
8 large eggs
1 teaspoon kosher salt
¼ teaspoon black pepper
¼ cup fresh basil or Italian flat-leaf parsley leaves, chopped
½ cup grated or crumbled cheese, such as cheddar, Swiss, feta, or Parmesan

INSTRUCTIONS
1. Turn the oven on and set it to 350 degrees.
2. Put the skillet on the stove, turn the heat to medium, and carefully add 1 teaspoon oil.
3. Add the onion and cook, stirring occasionally, until golden and softened, about 7 minutes. Turn the heat down to low, add the vegetables and potatoes, and cook until the vegetables are tender, 5 to 10 minutes. Set aside to cool, about 10 minutes.
4. Put the eggs, salt, and pepper in the mixing bowl and, using the fork or whisk, beat until the mixture is pale yellow.
5. Add the cooled onion mixture, basil or parsley, and cheese, and mix well.
6. Pour the mixture into the skillet and carefully put it in the oven.
7. Bake until the top is golden and the eggs are set, 25 to 30 minutes. (To see if the eggs are set, use the pot holders to jiggle the pan back and forth: the eggs should not move around in a liquidy way.)
8. Set aside to cool and serve warm or at room temperature. Or cover and refrigerate up to 2 days.

Fancy That!
- Instead of the broccoli or cauliflower, try adding a big handful of spinach or shredded kale, chopped asparagus, sliced zucchini, diced leftover sweet potatoes, even corn, frozen or cut fresh from the cob.
- Stir in ½ cup diced ham, sliced cooked sausages, or cooked bacon, crumbled. Or add some diced leftover turkey or chicken.

Our frittata is baked in the oven—making it easier to cook and healthier for you—but frittata actually comes from the Italian word for "fried"!

Breakfast Sandwiches

A grab-and-go breakfast sandwich is classic fast food—but we don't mean the restaurant kind. Breakfast sandwiches are so easy and so nourishing to make at home when you add your own ingredients. Mix and match fillings and toppings with the bread of your choice to make your own new classic—then name it after yourself!

INGREDIENTS

BASE +	PROTEIN +	VEGETABLE/FRUIT +	TOPPINGS
(Pick 1)	(Pick 1)	(Pick 2 or 3)	(Pick as many as you want)

BASE +
(Pick 1)

Whole-wheat bread

Multigrain bagel

Tortilla

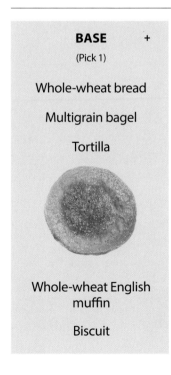

Whole-wheat English muffin

Biscuit

PROTEIN +
(Pick 1)

Sliced hard-cooked egg

Fried egg

Scrambled egg or wedge of frittata

Peanut or almond butter

Ham

VEGETABLE/FRUIT +
(Pick 2 or 3)

Tomatoes

Mushrooms or bell peppers

Avocado

Apple or banana slices

Spinach

TOPPINGS
(Pick as many as you want)

Hot sauce or salsa

Onions or scallions, greens and whites

Fresh herbs

Sliced or grated cheese

Lunch

Breakfast and dinner are the bookends around your day—the gearing-up meal and the winding-down meal. But lunch is different. Lunch is a pause in the middle of everything.

It's a moment to take a breath, sit down with your friends or your family, and recharge for whatever's next.

Lunch is an easy meal to make—a sandwich, a salad, or vegetables and dip—and since you're often taking it on the road, it's got to be an easy one to pack, too. So the key is to keep it exciting! Your mission is to stay out of the lunch rut (avoiding that same old sandwich you didn't even love the first 25 times you ate it) and learning some new recipes will help.

We'll show you how best to fill a lunchbox with sandwiches you'll actually want to eat, and how to fill those sandwiches with all your favorites, plus lots of fun add-ins and variations. We also have lots of tips and tricks to figure out what to do with what you already have (like leftover pasta), how to do some basic lunch equations (cottage cheese + strawberries = lunch), and how to whip up the best take-along dips. And when you've got a little more time on your hands, you can unwind over a nice, lazy weekend lunch.

Sandwich Mix-and-Match

Sure, lettuce and tomato are great, but there's a wide world of possibilities for sandwiches out there! Don't limit yourself to the usual, or even to what we suggest here. As long as you've got a good balance of protein and vegetables, textures and tastes, and a whole lot of colors, you're going to have a sandwich that satisfies your mouth's flavor cravings and your body's energy requirements.

INGREDIENTS

BASE +	**PROTEIN** +	**VEGETABLE** +	**FRUIT** +	**CONDIMENTS AND DIPS**
(Pick 1)	(Pick 1)	(Pick 2 or 3)	(Pick 1)	
Whole-wheat bread or toast	Chicken salad	Shredded carrots or purple cabbage	Sliced pears	Pesto
Wrap	Egg Salad (page 33) or sliced hard-cooked eggs	Greens, including romaine lettuce, mesclun, or spinach	Sliced grapes	Cucumber Tsatsiki (page 42)
Multigrain bagel			Sliced pineapple	Dijon mustard
Tortilla	Ham	Sliced radishes		Guacamole (page 42)
Whole-wheat English muffin		Avocado		Classic Hummus (page 41)
		Sliced tomato	Dried cranberries	
	Turkey	Oven-Roasted Vegetables (page 126)	Sliced apples	
Pita		Sprouts		Sliced pickles
Multigrain roll		Sliced cucumbers		Capers
Whole-wheat hamburger or hot-dog bun	Tuna Salad (page 35) or sardines		Sliced peaches	Jam or apple butter
	Cheese		Raisins	
	Peanut or almond butter		Sliced Banana	

Sandwiches/Wraps

Fifteen sandwiches to spark your imagination and taste buds!

1. Chicken and Brie cheese with apple slices and apple butter

2. Smoked turkey and sliced avocado with shredded carrots

3. Smoked ham and cheddar cheese with cucumber slices and mango chutney or apple butter

4. Smoked ham with cucumber slices, pineapple slices, and mustard

5. Tuna salad with sprouts, sliced radishes, and sliced grapes

6. Sardines with mashed avocado, cucumber slices, and tomato slices

7. Egg Salad (page 33) or sliced egg with sprouts and capers

8. Egg Salad (page 33) or sliced egg with Cucumber Tsatsiki (page 42)

9. Feta and Oven-Roasted Vegetables (page 126) with shredded carrots

10. Cheddar cheese and mashed avocado with tomato and pickles

11. Mozzarella cheese with tomato slices and pesto

12. Brie cheese with spinach leaves and sliced peaches

13. Classic Hummus (page 41) and Oven-Roasted Vegetables (page 126)

14. Classic Hummus (page 41) with cucumber slices and tomato slices

15. Peanut butter with apple slices, banana slices, and raisins

Who needs bread? A large lettuce leaf makes a great sandwich wrap. Be sure to use at least one filling that will hold everything together, such as Classic Hummus (page 41) or Guacamole (page 42), then lay the rest of the ingredients on top, tightly roll up your leaf, and munch away.

Hate soggy sandwiches? Everybody does. So do it differently:

- **Put a single layer** of meat or cheese on each slice of bread, spread the condiments on those, and then stuff the vegetables and the rest of the filling in the middle. The meat or cheese protects the bread from getting soggy.
- **Blot drippy sandwich ingredients** like tomatoes, pickles, and cucumbers on a paper towel before you add them.
- **Pack your sandwich in parts,** and assemble it at lunchtime. You'll need a lidded plastic container: start with the bread on the bottom, then layer your sandwich ingredients between pieces of waxed paper, and finish with a small container of any wet ingredients, such as mustard or hummus. Or assemble most of your sandwich, but leave out anything damp or wet, such as tomato or pickles, which you can pack separately. Don't forget a butter knife for spreading!

Quesadillas

A quesadilla is like a Mexican grilled cheese sandwich—using tortillas instead of bread. *Queso* (*kay*-so) actually means "cheese"! If you prefer corn tortillas, use two per quesadilla, sandwiching the cheese in the middle between them instead of folding them. *By Adam Ried*

ADULT NEEDED: YES · HANDS-ON TIME: 15 MINUTES · TOTAL TIME: 15 MINUTES · MAKES: 2 QUESADILLAS

KITCHEN GEAR
Cutting board
Measuring cup
Colander or strainer
Small mixing bowl
Wooden spoon
Sharp knife (adult needed)
Large nonstick skillet
Heatproof spatula
Large plate, for serving

INGREDIENTS
2 (8-inch) whole-grain tortillas
½ cup grated Monterey Jack or cheddar cheese
¼ cup canned or cooked black or pinto beans, drained and rinsed
¼ cup canned or frozen corn (drained or thawed as needed)
2 scallions, greens and whites, thinly sliced
Salsa (if you like)
Plain Greek yogurt (if you like)

INSTRUCTIONS
1. Put the tortillas on the cutting board and sprinkle half the cheese over half of each tortilla.
2. Put the beans, corn, and scallions in the mixing bowl, and mix well.
3. Sprinkle half the bean-and-corn mixture over the cheese on each tortilla, then fold the tortilla to make a half-moon shape.
4. Put the skillet on the stove and turn the heat to medium-low. Add the quesadillas. Use the spatula to press down gently. Cook, flipping halfway through, until they are spotty brown and crisp on both sides. The cheese inside should be melted.
5. Take them out of the skillet and let them cool about 2 minutes on the serving plate.
6. Cut into wedges and serve with salsa and Greek yogurt, if you like.

Fancy That!
Add ¼ cup of one or more of the following:
- sautéed zucchini slices or mushrooms
- sliced olives or radishes
- Guacamole (page 42) or diced avocados
- Oven-Roasted Vegetables (page 126)
- leftover chicken or turkey
- shredded carrots or cabbage
- loosely packed cilantro leaves

Hard-Cooked Eggs

There are many, many different methods for cooking hard-cooked eggs. You may have your own method, but why don't you take a crack at ours and see if you like it? We have a hunch you will! It's a foolproof method for hard-cooked eggs with tender whites and creamy yolks.

ADULT: YES • HANDS-ON TIME: 10 MINUTES • TOTAL TIME: 30 MINUTES • MAKES: 4 EGGS

KITCHEN GEAR
Medium-sized bowl
Medium-sized pot with lid
Kitchen timer
Slotted spoon or tongs

INGREDIENTS
4 large eggs

INSTRUCTIONS
1. Fill the bowl with cold tap water and add 6 to 8 ice cubes.
2. Gently lower the eggs into the pot and add enough water to cover the eggs by about 1 inch.
3. Put the pot on the stove, turn the heat to medium-high, and bring the water to a boil.
4. As soon as the water boils, turn off the heat, cover the pot, and let sit for 10 minutes.
5. Using the slotted spoon or tongs, gently move the hot eggs to the bowl of ice water and let them cool for 5 minutes.
6. Drain the eggs (hold them against the bowl with your hand while you pour out the water), then shake the bowl back and forth so the eggs roll around, bump into each other hard, and the shells crack all over. The cracked shells should be easy to peel off with your fingers—but sometimes they're not, so just do your best.

Egg Salad

If you're a fan of egg salad, you'll love this superfresh version, and if you're not, you're likely to change your mind.

ADULT NEEDED: YES • HANDS-ON TIME: 15 MINUTES • TOTAL TIME: 15 MINUTES • MAKES: 4 SERVINGS

KITCHEN GEAR
Cutting board
Sharp knife (adult needed)
Small bowl
Measuring spoons
Fork

INGREDIENTS
4 large eggs, hard-cooked and peeled (page 32)
1 celery stalk, minced
2 tablespoons plain Greek yogurt
1 tablespoon olive oil, or an additional 1
    tablespoon yogurt
1 teaspoon mustard (any kind is fine)
1 tablespoon chopped fresh herbs, such as
    parsley, basil, dill, tarragon, or cilantro, plus extra
    for garnish (if you like)
⅛ teaspoon kosher salt

INSTRUCTIONS
1. Cut the eggs in half lengthwise and then cut them a few more times (they don't need to be evenly cut). Put them in the bowl.
2. Add the celery, yogurt, olive oil or additional yogurt, mustard, herbs, and salt and, using the fork, mash until still chunky or creamy, whichever you prefer.
3. Serve right away or cover and refrigerate up to 1 day.

Fancy That!
Curried Egg Salad: Add 1 teaspoon curry powder and 1 tablespoon chopped fresh cilantro or basil leaves
Lemony Egg Salad: Add 1 teaspoon fresh lemon juice and 1 teaspoon lemon zest
Herby Egg Salad: Add minced scallions or radishes and double the herbs

Try This

Eggs are fragile, right? If you drop one, you'll know for sure. But what if you squeeze one as hard as you can? Try it. Hold an egg (in the shell, of course!) in the palm of your hand, wrap your fingers around it, and squeeze. Did it break? We didn't think so! That's because an egg is like a 3-D version of an arch, which is one of the strongest shapes in architecture. The curved form of the shell spreads the pressure evenly all over, rather than concentrating it at any one point.

Why do you turn the heat off when you are cooking eggs? Even if the stove is off, the hot water continues to cook the egg. If you leave the heat on, the eggs will cook too much and be tough.

After cooking, why do you put the eggs in ice water? The ice water prevents the eggs from overcooking.

Deviled Eggs

This is like an inside-out version of our egg salad! If you want to make these eggs truly devilish, just add a little bit of hot sauce.

ADULT NEEDED: YES • HANDS-ON TIME: 15 MINUTES • TOTAL TIME: 15 MINUTES • MAKES: 4 SERVINGS

KITCHEN GEAR
Cutting board
Sharp knife (adult needed)
Measuring spoons
Small bowl
Fork
Plate
Spoon

INGREDIENTS
2 tablespoons plain Greek yogurt
1 teaspoon mustard (any kind is fine)
1 tablespoon chopped fresh herbs, such as parsley, basil, dill, tarragon, or cilantro, plus extra for garnish (if you like)
⅛ teaspoon kosher salt
4 large eggs, hard-cooked and peeled (page 32)

INSTRUCTIONS
1. Put the yogurt, mustard, herbs, and salt in the bowl and set aside.
2. Cut the eggs in half lengthwise. Remove the yolks (they'll pop out if you push the white underneath them) and put them in the bowl with the yogurt mixture and mash until chunky or creamy, whichever you prefer.
3. Put the whites on the plate. Use a spoon to refill each egg half with the yolk mixture and sprinkle with extra herbs, if you like.

DID YOU KNOW?

Capers are the salted and pickled flower buds of the caper bush. They taste like peppery green olives, but they have a softer texture.

Be Creative
Add any of these to the yolk mixture:
Italian Eggs: Add 1 tablespoon drained capers, 1 teaspoon olive paste, and 1 anchovy filet, chopped
Curried Eggs: Add ½ teaspoon curry powder plus 1 tablespoon mango chutney

Tuna Salad

Tuna with mayo is tasty, but here's a fresh idea that uses tangy yogurt instead. Love lemon? Add some grated lemon zest to increase the citrus flavor.

ADULT NEEDED: YES • HANDS-ON TIME: 20 MINUTES • TOTAL TIME: 20 MINUTES • MAKES: 2 ½ CUPS

KITCHEN GEAR
Can opener
Small bowl
Fork
Measuring spoons
Measuring cup
Sharp knife (adult needed)

INGREDIENTS
2   (5-ounce) cans tuna (any kind is fine), drained
3   tablespoons plain Greek or regular plain yogurt
1   tablespoon fresh lemon juice
¼   cup minced celery (about 1 stalk)
1   tablespoon minced fresh herb leaves, like dill, basil, or cilantro
1   tablespoon olive oil
½   teaspoon mustard (any kind is fine)

INSTRUCTIONS
1. Drain the tuna and put it in the bowl and break up the clumps with the fork.
2. Add the yogurt, lemon juice, celery, herbs, olive oil, and mustard and mix well.
3. Cover and refrigerate at least 1 hour and up to 3 days to let the flavors mingle.

Zest is the outer, colorful skin of the citrus fruit.

Curry powder is a South Asian seasoning blend—a mixture of spices that usually includes coriander, red pepper, turmeric, cumin, and up to a dozen others!

Fancy That!
Try adding one of the following:
- 1 apple, washed, cored, and chopped, and 2 teaspoons relish or chopped pickles (sweet or dill)
- ¼ cup currants, raisins, or dried cranberries and 2 teaspoons curry powder
- ½ cup sliced seedless grapes and 1 tablespoon chopped fresh dill
- ¼ cup chopped red onion, 10 chopped black and/or green olives (pitted, of course), and ½ cup chopped roasted red peppers
- 1 cucumber and 1 red bell pepper, both diced, and 1 carrot, shredded

Chicken Salad

Leftover roast chicken makes great chicken salad—and chicken salad makes a tasty sandwich filling or green-salad topper! Once you taste the basic recipe, you'll get a good idea of where you might want to take the flavor next time.

ADULT NEEDED: YES • ACTIVE TIME: 15 MINUTES • TOTAL TIME: 15 MINUTES • MAKES: 6 CUPS

KITCHEN GEAR
Large mixing bowl
Measuring cup
Large spoon
Measuring spoons
Sharp knife (adult needed)

DID YOU KNOW?

Dried herbs are stronger and more concentrated than fresh herbs. 1 tablespoon fresh equals 1 teaspoon dried.

INGREDIENTS
4–4 ½ cups shredded cooked chicken
¼ cup mayonnaise
¼ cup plain yogurt
1 teaspoon white vinegar or fresh lemon juice
1 tablespoon Dijon mustard
1 apple (any kind is fine), washed, cored, and diced
1 celery stalk, diced

INSTRUCTIONS
1. Put the mayonnaise, yogurt, vinegar or lemon juice, and mustard in the bowl and mix well.
2. Add the chicken, apple, and celery and mix to combine.
3. Serve right away or cover and refrigerate overnight.

Fancy That!

- Add 1 tablespoon curry powder, ¼ cup raisins or chopped dried apricots, and ¼ cup chopped toasted walnuts or pecans
- Add 1 tablespoon fresh or 1 teaspoon dried tarragon or basil leaves

EXPERT: Mayonnaise/Aioli

Are you an expert, ready to move on to something more complex? Homemade mayonnaise is silkier and tastier than store-bought, so we encourage you to make your own. The French call it aioli (eye-*oh*-lee), which really just means oil and garlic, and scientists call it an emulsion.

ADULT NEEDED: NO • HANDS-ON TIME: 15 MINUTES • TOTAL TIME: 15 MINUTES • MAKES: 2 ½ CUPS

KITCHEN GEAR
Food processor or blender (adult needed)
Measuring spoons
Measuring cup
Jar with lid

INGREDIENTS
1 garlic clove, peeled
½ teaspoon kosher salt
2 tablespoons fresh lemon juice
2 large egg yolks
1 teaspoon water
½ cup canola or vegetable oil
½ cup olive oil

INSTRUCTIONS
1. Put the garlic and salt in the food processor fitted with a steel blade. Put the top on tightly and pulse until well chopped but not minced.
2. Add the lemon juice and egg yolks and process until well mixed.
3. While the machine is running, add the water through the feeding tube at the top, and then gradually add the canola and olive oils, 1 tablespoon at a time, and process until smooth and thick. (The water is needed to keep the oil droplets separated. If you add the oil too fast, there is not enough time for the oil to break into small droplets.)
4. Pour the mixture into the jar. Cover and refrigerate at least 1 hour and up to 3 days.

Dips and Spreads

Everybody loves dip: It's just plain fun to interact with your food, especially when it's so tasty. Of course, if you're dipping potato chips into sour cream, you're going to have to stop pretty quickly, since neither food has much to offer, nutritionally speaking. But if you make one of the delicious dips in this chapter and serve it with some veggies and whole-wheat crackers—well, dip all you want. In fact, you can go ahead and serve it for lunch or dinner if you like! There's no rule that says that a meal means hot things on a plate, after all.

White Bean Dip

When you puree beans, they make a rich, creamy dip that's delicious with French bread, pita chips, or raw vegetables. Or use it instead of mayonnaise, as a spread for a ham or cheese sandwich—it will add lots more flavor and nutrients.

ADULT NEEDED: YES • HANDS-ON TIME: 15 MINUTES • TOTAL TIME: 15 MINUTES • MAKES: 1 ¼ CUPS

KITCHEN GEAR
Can opener
Measuring cup
Colander or strainer
Food processor (adult needed)
Sharp knife (adult needed)
Measuring spoons
Large spoon
Serving bowl

INGREDIENTS
2 cups cooked or canned white beans, drained and rinsed
1–2 garlic cloves, peeled and minced or chopped
¼ cup olive oil
3 tablespoons fresh lemon juice (about 1 lemon)
½ teaspoon kosher salt
¼ teaspoon black pepper

INSTRUCTIONS
1. Put the white beans, garlic, oil, lemon juice, salt, and pepper in the food processor fitted with a steel blade. Put the top on tightly and process until completely smooth. (If you don't have a food processor, you can mash everything using a fork or a potato masher. It won't get as smooth but it will definitely be yummy!)
2. Spoon into the serving bowl, cover, and refrigerate at least 1 hour and up to 2 days.

Fancy That!
When you add the beans, add one or more of these:
- 1–2 tablespoons chopped fresh basil, parsley, or cilantro leaves, or snipped chives
- 1 teaspoon chopped fresh rosemary
- 1 teaspoon lemon zest
- 1–2 tablespoons chopped or pureed olives
- 1 teaspoon chopped jalapeño peppers or hot sauce (if you like it spicy)
- 1 tablespoon pesto

Be Creative
Substitute black beans for the white beans, and lime for the lemon.

Note: Don't worry if you run out of carrot and celery sticks! Not only are there loads of other great veggies (bell pepper strips, asparagus, cherry tomatoes, cucumber slices), but dips also make great sandwich fillings, roll-up spreads, and burger toppings.

 **DID YOU KNOW?** Ounce for ounce, beans have more protein than beef.

How to Use a Can Opener

1. Set the can on a flat, hard surface.

2. Pull apart the two handles of the can opener.

3. Flip the can opener over and look at the two wheels on the bottom of the opener. One is jagged (bumpy on the edges) and one is smooth on the edges.

4. With the help of your adult, place the smooth (cutting) wheel against the inside of the little rim at the top of the can and close the two handles.

5. Hold both handles in your left hand and place your right hand (lefties, go left) on the little winglike part of the can opener.

6. Slowly twist the wing with your free hand while squeezing the handles closed with your other hand. This should start cutting into the can's lid and rolling around its edge.

7. Continue to turn the wing until the can opener has gone all the way around the top off the can.

8. Pull apart the handles of the opener.

9. Carefully lift out the lid of the can (you may need to pry it out with a fork), rinse it off, and toss it in your recycling bin.

Classic Hummus
with an Endless List of Variations

Here's a bean dip that you're probably familiar with: hummus, the classic Middle Eastern dip of chickpeas, sesame tahini, garlic, and lemon juice. Once you start making it yourself, you will be really surprised that anyone buys it in a container! We love to add this to turkey and ham sandwiches, or to our burgers!

ADULT NEEDED: YES · HANDS-ON TIME: 15 MINUTES · TOTAL TIME: 15 MINUTES · MAKES: 1 ½ CUPS

KITCHEN GEAR
Can opener
Colander or strainer
Food processor (adult needed)
Measuring spoons
Rubber spatula or large spoon
Serving bowl

INGREDIENTS
1 (16-ounce) can chickpeas (garbanzo beans), drained and rinsed with cold tap water
2–3 garlic cloves, peeled and minced or chopped
3 tablespoons sesame tahini
1 tablespoon olive oil
3 tablespoons fresh lemon juice
½ teaspoon ground cumin, or more (if you like)
½ teaspoon kosher salt
¼ teaspoon black pepper
Lemon, lime, or orange slices, for garnish

INSTRUCTIONS
1. Put the chickpeas and garlic in the food processor fitted with a steel blade. Put the top on tightly and process until well chopped.
2. Gradually, through the feeding tube on top, add the tahini, oil, lemon juice, cumin, salt, and pepper and process again until completely smooth. If the hummus isn't creamy, add hot water, 1 tablespoon at a time, and process until it is.
3. Spoon into the serving bowl, cover, and refrigerate up to 2 days or serve right away garnished with lemon slices.

Be Creative
Try adding one of the following when you process the hummus:
- ½ cup chopped fresh basil, cilantro, or mint leaves
- ¼ cup chopped scallions, green and whites, or chives
- ½ cup chopped roasted bell pepper
- 1 tablespoon minced fresh chili peppers or ¼ teaspoon cayenne pepper
- ½ cup pitted green or black olives
- 1 tablespoon grated lemon, lime, or orange zest

Cucumber Tsatsiki

Tsatsiki is a tangy yogurt-based dip from Greece that's great with raw vegetables and pita chips, or spread on tomato sandwiches and all kinds of burgers (especially the Beanie Burger, page 106), spooned onto a piece of grilled fish, or even mixed into a salad instead of salad dressing.

ADULT NEEDED: YES • HANDS-ON TIME: 20 MINUTES • TOTAL TIME: 20 MINUTES • MAKES: 4 SERVINGS

KITCHEN GEAR
Cutting board
Sharp knife (adult needed)
Measuring cup
Small bowl

INGREDIENTS
1 small English cucumber or 1 conventional cucumber, peeled, thinly sliced and chopped

1 cup plain Greek yogurt (the thickest you can find)

1 garlic clove, peeled and minced

¼ cup finely chopped fresh mint leaves, plus extra for garnish (if you like)

¼ teaspoon kosher salt

INSTRUCTIONS
1. Put the cucumber, yogurt, garlic, mint, and salt in the mixing bowl and mix well.

2. Cover and refrigerate at least 1 hour and up to overnight. Serve garnished with the additional mint, if you like.

Guacamole

This is the classic, pale-green Mexican dip that makes the most of avocadoes' creaminess. Serve it with tortilla chips, pita chips, or on Beanie Burgers (page 106), Quesadillas (page 30), or a bowl of Vegetable Chili (page 112).

ADULT NEEDED: YES • HANDS-ON TIME: 20 MINUTES • TOTAL TIME: 20 MINUTES • MAKES: ABOUT 1 ½ CUPS

KITCHEN GEAR
Sharp knife (adult needed)
Cutting board
Spoon
Small bowl
Fork
Measuring spoons
Serving bowl

INGREDIENTS
2 ripe Hass avocadoes

½ small tomato, coarsely chopped

1 scallion, greens and whites chopped

1 heaping tablespoon finely chopped fresh cilantro leaves

2 teaspoons fresh lime or lemon juice

¼ teaspoon kosher salt

½–1 teaspoon hot sauce, if you like it spicy

INSTRUCTIONS
1. Slice each avocado in half (this is really a job for an adult). Remove the pit and use a spoon to scoop out the insides. Put the avocado in the bowl and using the fork, mash it until it is still a little bit chunky.

2. Add the tomato, scallion, cilantro, lime or lemon juice, and salt. Mash a bit more, but keep it chunky (unless you like it smooth). Add hot sauce, if you like it spicy.

3. Spoon the guacamole into the serving bowl and serve right away.

There are two main kinds of avocadoes: the bright green, smooth-skinned kind that are grown in Florida; and the dark-green or black, pebbly skinned kind, Hass, that are grown in California. We prefer Hass because the flesh is smoother, denser, and creamier.

Date-Nut Cream Cheese

This spread makes a delicious and nutritious filling for anything, from a sandwich to a celery stick. For a different taste, skip the cream cheese and stir the ingredients into peanut or almond butter instead.

ADULT NEEDED: NO • HANDS-ON TIME: 10 MINUTES • TOTAL TIME: 10 MINUTES • MAKES: 4 SERVINGS

KITCHEN GEAR
Clean kitchen scissors
Measuring cup
Measuring spoons
Small bowl
Fork

INGREDIENTS
7   dates or ¼ cup raisins, dried cranberries, or currants
4   ounces cream cheese (at room temperature)
1   tablespoon buttermilk or plain yogurt
¼   cup chopped toasted walnuts

INSTRUCTIONS
1. Pit the dates (if you use dates), then cut them up with a clean pair of kitchen scissors.
2. Put the cream cheese and buttermilk or yogurt in the bowl and, using the fork, mash until it is smooth.
3. Add the dates (or dried fruit) and walnuts and mash until the mixture is combined.
4. Serve right away or cover and refrigerate up to 3 days.

Homemade Peanut Butter

You'll be amazed how easy it is to make your own peanut butter from whole peanuts. It tastes great because it's so fresh, and it doesn't have any of the added sugar or oil that most store-bought peanut butter contains. If you like, try adding a pinch of cayenne pepper for spice, or a pinch of cinnamon for warmth.

ADULT NEEDED: YES · HANDS-ON TIME: 3 MINUTES · TOTAL TIME: 3 MINUTES · MAKES: 1 CUP, ENOUGH FOR ABOUT 8 SANDWICHES

KITCHEN GEAR
Measuring cup
Measuring spoons
Food processor (adult needed)
Rubber spatula
Spoon
Container with lid

INGREDIENTS
2 cups roasted peanuts
A pinch to ¼ teaspoon kosher salt (less for salted peanuts, more for unsalted)

INSTRUCTIONS
1. Put the peanuts in the food processor fitted with a steel blade. Put the top on tightly and process until they break down and bunch up into a glob that goes around in the food processor bowl, about 1 minute.
2. Stop the food processor, take off the top, and carefully scrape around the inside of the bowl with the spatula. Add the salt, put the top back on, and continue to process, stopping 2 or 3 more times to scrape the bowl, until the peanut butter is smooth, about 1 minute longer.
3. Scrape the peanut butter into the container. Cover and refrigerate up to 2 weeks. When you take the peanut butter out of the fridge, it will be a little bit hard and difficult to spread, but it will soften after a few minutes at room temperature. If you want to speed up the softening, pack it in a microwave-safe container and microwave for 5 to 10 seconds.

Why does the oil separate from the nuts? The oil is less dense than the solids in the nut butter, so it slowly rises to the top. In the refrigerator, the oil freezes into many tiny crystals, which hold the peanut butter together.

Why do nuts become oily when turned into butter? The oil in nuts is trapped inside tiny droplets. When you blend the nuts, these droplets break open and spill their oil, which coats the remaining nut fragments and forms a paste.

DID YOU KNOW?

Peanuts are native to the Americas, and were being mashed into a paste by the Aztecs hundreds of years ago. As for more modern versions, U.S. Patent 306,727 was issued in 1884 to Marcellus Gilmore Edson for his special method of milling roasted peanuts into a spreadable state.

Lunch Bowls

Lunch doesn't have to be complicated! Start with a bowlful of something simple, and it can only get better from there—especially when you add your favorite ingredients and toppings. Plus, they make great packable meals for your lunchbox—even if you'll be eating it out of a thermos and not a bowl.

Yogurt or Cottage-Cheese Bowl

Yogurt and cottage cheese both love the company of fruit or vegetables. Add any of the following combinations to ½ cup plain yogurt or cottage cheese.

Fruit Mix-Ins:

- Grapefruit sections, dried cranberries, and toasted almonds
- Fresh apricots, dried apricots, and a pinch of cinnamon
- Fresh (or frozen) berries and spoonful of Granola (page 10)
- Dried dates and toasted walnuts

- Pineapple and unsweetened dried coconut
- Fresh peaches, raspberries, and toasted pecans
- Grated apple and real maple syrup

Vegetable Mix-Ins:

- Thinly sliced cucumbers, grated or sliced radishes, and fresh mint leaves
- Grated carrots and baby spinach
- Sliced celery and olives
- Shredded purple cabbage, grated zucchini, and fresh dill

Pasta or Grain Bowl

Turn leftover rice, pasta, barley, or quinoa into lunch. Basically, you're making pasta (or grain) salad right in your bowl! Start with 1 cup cooked pasta or grain, warm it a little first (30 seconds in the microwave is perfect), then add some of the following, along with a teaspoon each of olive oil and lemon juice, and salt to taste—or a splash of salad dressing. If you're going for more of an Asian flavor, try adding a teaspoon each of soy sauce and rice vinegar, and ½ teaspoon sesame oil.

Mix-Ins

- Crumbled feta cheese, chopped tomatoes, and fresh dill
- Shrimp and pesto
- Tuna, broccoli, and raisins
- Chickpeas, chopped roasted bell peppers, and curry powder

- Pinto beans, cheddar cheese, chopped tomatoes, and cilantro
- Cooked edamame, shredded Napa cabbage, and sliced scallions, greens and whites
- Blue cheese, baby spinach, and chopped red onion
- Cubed mozzarella cheese, chopped tomatoes, fresh basil, and pine nuts
- Crumbled feta cheese, avocado cubes, sliced radishes, and toasted pumpkin seeds
- Spoonful Cucumber Tsatsiki (page 42), peas (fresh or frozen), and cherry tomatoes
- Spoonful Classic Hummus (page 41), diced cucumbers, and fresh mint
- Grated Parmesan cheese, sliced mushrooms, and fresh basil
- Baked tofu, steamed broccoli, and peanuts or sesame seeds

Soups

Soup is a whole meal in a bowl, and it's one of the most useful and versatile things you can learn how to make. For starters, soup is a terrific occasion for creativity—you can mix and match as you please.

Don't take our word for it: if you love zucchini but we don't suggest it as an ingredient, add it to your version and see what you think. Suppose we suggest dill but you love basil; try basil instead. If we suggest chunky and you like smooth, whip out your blender. You can also test out different herbs and seasonings, or try to re-create the flavor of a favorite soup you've had at a friend's house or a favorite restaurant. Soup is a great opportunity to use up whatever odds and ends you have in the fridge: A single carrot adds a little sweetness. Two potatoes add a creamy texture. Half a bunch of greens that are about to wilt? Sure! As long as they are fresh, add them to the pot.

There are hundreds—probably thousands—of kinds of soup, but we're going to teach you a few basic recipes that will set you up for creating your own version. First, chicken soup. The traditional method starts with a whole chicken, and if your grandmother makes chicken soup from scratch, this is probably how she makes it. Perfect. Grandma's got that covered. Because the other, quicker, easier, and more kid-friendly method starts with sautéed vegetables, boneless (or leftover) chicken, and boxed broth. We'll show you how to make this basic chicken soup, and then we'll show you lots and lots of variations so you can mix it up and make it taste the way you want it to. Or experiment to discover new and wild flavors!

Next, there's vegetable soup, which is really a variation on chicken soup, except that it uses way more vegetables and, well, no chicken. But for the most part, the instructions are the same. Vegetable soups can be creamy (which means pureed with or without the addition of milk, yogurt, or cream) or chunky. Some people like their vegetable soup to be creamy-chunky, which means just what it sounds like: a portion of it is pureed and then added back to the unpureed soup.

Vegetable soups are the easiest, most varied, and most versatile soups of all. Most can be made from start to finish in less than an hour, many can be created from what you've already got in the fridge or pantry, and almost all lend themselves to creative substitutions and additions.

Bean soup follows the same basic instructions but—can you guess?—with the addition of beans. There are a lot of different kinds of beans and some can be substituted for others. But there are a few bean soups that really require specific beans. Bean soups are a great thing to know how to make because they're nourishing, filling, inexpensive, and really yummy (plus they freeze well).

We're including quick breads in this chapter, too, because they add just the right something to turn a bowl of soup into dinner.

Soup Basics

Mirepoix (meer-*pwa*)

It sounds like a French cathedral, but *mirepoix* is just a mixture of onion, carrots, and celery that we start almost all our soups with. Why do we always do that? Heating that particular trio of vegetables causes chemical reactions that give them a brown color and a rich, caramelized taste. Once you add the liquid, all that good flavor dissolves into your soup!

Broth

You can buy chicken broth in cans or boxes. Look for broth labeled "low-sodium" and/or "all-natural": these versions won't have additives in them, like MSG (monosodium glutamate, a type of salt), which can be unhealthy and make your soup taste odd.

Why low-sodium broth? Because too much salt isn't good for you and it doesn't taste good. Plus, it's better for you to decide how much salt you want rather than depend on the broth company to get it just right.

Garnishing

Garnishing (decorating with something edible) the bowl of soup does more than fancy up simple food—although  it does do that. It can also add an important burst of flavor or even a bit of texture. Croutons add crunch to a bowl of gazpacho; a sprinkle of fresh herbs adds flavor and color to almost any soup; a splash of lemon, vinegar, or even vinaigrette makes a bean soup taste more vibrant. Experiment and see.

Soup Mix-Ins

Make it rich: a drizzle of olive oil or a spoonful of pesto

Make it creamy: a spoonful of plain yogurt or sour cream, or a swirl of cream

Make it cheesy: a sprinkle of grated Parmesan or cheddar cheese

Make it crunchy: a few Croutons (page 85) or toasted nuts or seeds

Make it tangy: a squeeze or slice of lemon or lime, a dash of vinegar, or a splash of vinaigrette

Make it fresh: a snip or sprig of an herb such as parsley, basil, cilantro, chives, or dill

Make it spicy: a dash of hot sauce, sliced jalapeños, chili sauce, or chili flakes

Basic Chicken Soup

This quick and easy chicken soup is a great place to begin. Once you have mastered it, you can start making almost any other soup with ease. Try this even when time is short: you'll feel like an accomplished and brilliant chef.

ADULT NEEDED: YES • HANDS-ON TIME: 20 MINUTES • TOTAL TIME: 1 ½ HOURS • MAKES: 10–12 CUPS

KITCHEN GEAR

Large heavy-bottomed pot
Measuring cup
Measuring spoons
Sharp knife (adult needed)
Cutting board
Pot holder
Ladle

INGREDIENTS

1 tablespoon olive, canola, or vegetable oil
1 onion, finely chopped
2 celery stalks, sliced
2 carrots, scrubbed or peeled, and sliced
8 cups low-sodium chicken broth
½ cup rice, barley, or small pasta (such as alphabets or orzo)
¾–1 pound boneless, skinless chicken breasts or thighs, cooked and shredded

INSTRUCTIONS

1. Put the pot on the stove and turn the heat to medium. When it is hot, carefully add the oil.
2. Add the onion, celery, and carrots, and cook until tender, 10 to 15 minutes.
3. Add the chicken broth, raise the heat to high, and bring to a boil. Turn the heat down to low and cook, uncovered, until the vegetables no longer float on the top, about 30 minutes.
4. Add the rice and cook until tender, about 20 minutes. (If you want, use leftover grains or pasta. If so, skip this step and add them when you add the chicken in step 5. This will also cut 20 minutes off the cooking time.)
5. Add the chicken, stir, and cook until heated throughout, about 3 minutes.
6. Serve right away, or cover and refrigerate up to 3 days.

SAFETY ! TIP

A skillet usually takes one to three minutes to heat up, depending on your stove. If you're not sure, carefully drop some water in the skillet: if it sizzles, the skillet is hot. **Don't test the pan by touching it:** You'll get burned!

Fancy That!

Lemony Chicken Soup: Add 1 bay leaf and 1 strip lemon zest when you add the broth. Remove both before serving.

Herby Chicken Soup: Add 1 teaspoon dried marjoram (or 1 tablespoon chopped fresh), 1 teaspoon dried rosemary (or 1 tablespoon chopped fresh), and ¼ teaspoon dried thyme (or 1 teaspoon chopped fresh). If you're using dried herbs, add them when you cook the vegetables. If you're using fresh herbs, stir them in right before serving the soup.

Garlicky Ginger Soup: Add 1 tablespoon chopped fresh ginger and 2 garlic cloves, minced or chopped, when you add the onion.

Curried Chicken Soup: When you sauté the onion, add 1 Granny Smith apple, cored and cubed, 1 to 2 tablespoons curry powder, and 1 tomato, cubed. Stir in ¼ cup unsweetened, shredded coconut and 2 tablespoons chopped cilantro leaves just before serving.

Lettuce Eat Chicken Soup: Add 6 romaine lettuce or spinach leaves, chopped, when you add the rice, barley, or pasta, and ½ cup grated Parmesan cheese just before serving.

Tortilla Soup: Skip the rice, barley, or pasta and stir in ¼ cup chopped cilantro, the juice of ½ lime, and a handful of tortilla chips just before serving.

Tortellini Soup: Add cooked tortellini instead of the rice, barley, or small pasta.

EXPERT: **Matzo Balls**

Matzo balls are like Jewish dumplings, and they're delicious. They expand a lot when you cook them, so don't be tempted to make them bigger than this!

ADULT NEEDED: YES • HANDS-ON TIME: 30 MINUTES • TOTAL TIME: 2 HOURS • MAKES: 12–16 MATZO BALLS

KITCHEN GEAR
Large bowl
Whisk or egg beater
Medium-sized bowl
Measuring spoons
Measuring cup
Large pot
Slotted spoon

INGREDIENTS:
6   large eggs, at
      room temperature
      and separated
1 ½ teaspoons
      kosher salt
1   cup plus 2
      tablespoons
      matzo meal

INSTRUCTIONS
1. Put the egg whites in the large bowl and, using the whisk or egg beater, beat until stiff (it will stand up and look like a peak in the center). You might want to get help from an adult or another kid; whisking eggs can take a while and tire out your hand. Set aside.
2. Put the egg yolks and salt in the other bowl and beat until bright yellow and creamy.
3. Add the matzo meal to the bowl with the egg yolks and combine well.
4. Add the yolk-matzo mixture to the egg whites and combine well.
5. Cover and refrigerate at least 45 minutes and up to overnight.
6. Divide into 12 to 16 portions and form into balls.
7. Put a large pot of water on the stove and turn the heat to high.
8. Bring to a boil and add the chilled matzo balls. When the water returns to a boil, turn the heat down to low and cook for 45 minutes.
9. Carefully remove the matzo balls with the slotted spoon and gently lower them into soup bowls. Add the hot chicken soup and serve right away.

Why is it important to have the egg whites free of the yolks? The protein molecules in the egg white stick together to form a net, which traps air bubbles. The fat in the yolks makes this structure weak, as if you replaced some of your Legos with Jell-O.

Why do you need to chill the matzo ball mixture? Chilling the matzo balls allows them to keep their shape while they cook.

Vegetable Soups

Making vegetable soup is a great way to satisfy a belly that needs filling—but it's also useful for managing a thriving garden, a generous zucchini-growing neighbor, or a fridge full of odds and ends (just be sure they are fresh).

In the recipes that follow, we rarely specify cups, calling instead for pounds or a number of whole carrots or a head of broccoli—that way you don't have to fiddle around so much with measuring while you're prepping the ingredients. Plus, we want you to feel free to adjust to your tastes. Don't worry about being exact. Making soup is like a fun science project: you can experiment and figure out what you like and what works. If you find that a soup is too thick because, for example, the broccoli head is larger than expected, simply add more broth.

Here are some general equivalents, in case you've got baseball-bat-sized zucchini or marble-sized potatoes, and you want to know how much to use:

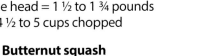

Asparagus
1 average bunch = 1 pound,
trimmed = 3 ½ cups trimmed and chopped

Broccoli
1 average head = 1 ½ to 1 ¾ pounds
= 4 ½ to 5 cups chopped

Butternut squash
1 large = 2 to 2 ½ pounds
= 5 cups chopped

Carrots
1 medium = 1/6 pound = ¾ cup chopped

Cauliflower
1 medium head = 2 to 2 ½ pounds
= 5 to 6 cups chopped

Corn
1 medium ear = ½ to ¾ cup kernels

Mushrooms
1 pound = 6 to 7 cups trimmed and sliced

Sweet potatoes
1 medium = ½ to ¾ pound
= 2 to 2 ½ cups diced

Summer squash
1 medium = ½ pound = 1 ½ to 2 cups diced

Tomatoes
1 medium = ½ pound = 1 cup diced

Zucchini
1 medium = ½ pound = 1 ¾ cups sliced

(Almost) **Any-Vegetable Soup**

This recipe works for almost any vegetable. You can also combine vegetables, if that's your fancy. If you like soup with a thick, creamy texture, add the rice or potato when you puree it.

ADULT NEEDED: YES • HANDS-ON TIME: 15 MINUTES • TOTAL TIME: 2 ½ HOURS • MAKES: 6–8 SERVINGS

KITCHEN GEAR
Large heavy-bottomed pot
Measuring cup
Measuring spoons
Sharp knife (adult needed)
Cutting board
Slotted spoon
Blender or food processor (adult needed)
Pot holder
Clean dish towel
Ladle
Container with lid

INGREDIENTS
1 tablespoon olive, canola, or vegetable oil or unsalted butter
1 large onion, coarsely chopped or thinly sliced
1 carrot, scrubbed or peeled, and chopped
1 celery stalk, sliced
1 garlic clove, peeled and minced or chopped
2–2 ½ pounds additional carrots; or butternut, winter, or summer squash; or button mushrooms; or 1 bunch celery; or 2 (28-ounce) cans whole tomatoes
8 cups low-sodium chicken broth
¼ cup brown rice or 1 potato, scrubbed and cubed (if you like)

SAFETY ! TIP

We are very serious about creating a way for the **steam to escape** when pureeing hot soup. There are four important steps:
1. Be sure to have the help of an adult.
2. Make sure the soup has cooled a bit.
3. Do not fill the blender all the way; fill it halfway at most.
4. Be sure you leave a way for steam to escape (see step 5 and 6 above).

INSTRUCTIONS
1. Put the pot on the stove and turn the heat to medium. When it is hot, carefully add the oil or butter.
2. Add the onion, carrot, celery, garlic, and the vegetables you have chosen and cook, stirring frequently, until tender, about 15 minutes.
3. Add the chicken broth and the rice or potato, if using. Raise the heat to high and bring to a boil.
4. Turn the heat down to low and cook, uncovered, for 45 minutes. Set aside to cool for 20 minutes at room temperature.
5. Very carefully, remove 2 cups of the vegetables and 1 cup liquid from the soup and put them in the blender. Do not fill the blender more than halfway.
6. If using a blender, put the top on but remove the little cap in the center (this will allow the steam to escape). Cover the cap hole with a clean dish towel. Turn the blender to the lowest speed and increase the blender speed as the soup purees. (If using a food processor, leave the plunger out while you puree the soup.)
7. As soon as the soup is pureed, pour it into another pot or an airtight storage container. Repeat this same process until all the soup has been pureed. If you need to reheat the soup, pour it back into the pot and reheat over low.
8. Serve right away, or cover and refrigerate up to 3 days.

DID YOU KNOW?

Cooking soup in a heavy-bottomed pot is important because the temperature will stay more uniform and constant as the soup cooks, and it will help prevent burning and sticking, two things that are sure to ruin your soup!

Broccoli/Cauliflower or Corn Soup

The only difference between this recipe and (Almost) Any-Vegetable Soup (page 58) is that these vegetables get added later in the cooking process. For broccoli, and cauliflower soup, you need to cook the vegetables a short time or they get stinky, mushy, and generally taste terrible (it's a taste we can't describe and hope you never have to experience!). For the corn, if you add it too soon, it will be mushy.

ADULT NEEDED: YES · HANDS-ON TIME: 15 MINUTES · TOTAL TIME: 2 ½ HOURS · MAKES: 6–8 SERVINGS

KITCHEN GEAR
Large heavy-bottomed pot
Measuring cup
Measuring spoons
Sharp knife (adult needed)
Cutting board
Slotted spoon
Blender or food processor (adult needed)
Pot holder
Clean dish towel
Ladle
Large container

INGREDIENTS
1 tablespoon olive, canola, or vegetable oil or unsalted butter
1 large onion, coarsely chopped or thinly sliced
1 carrot, scrubbed or peeled, and chopped
1 celery stalk, sliced
1 garlic clove, peeled and minced or chopped
1 head broccoli or cauliflower, chopped, or 4 cups fresh corn kernels
8 cups low-sodium chicken or vegetable broth
¼ cup brown rice or 1 potato, scrubbed and cubed (if you like)

INSTRUCTIONS
1. Put the pot on the stove and turn the heat to medium. When it is hot, carefully add the oil or butter.
2. Add the onion, carrot, celery, and garlic, and cook until tender, 10 to 15 minutes.
3. Add the chicken broth, the rice or potato, if using, raise the heat to high, and bring to a boil.
4. Turn the heat down to low and cook, uncovered, for 20 minutes. Add the vegetable you have chosen and cook until tender but firm, about 15 minutes, depending on the vegetable. Set aside and cool for 20 minutes.
5. Very carefully, remove 1 cup of the vegetables and 1 cup liquid from the soup and put them in the blender. Do not fill it more than halfway (you may want to leave the corn soup chunky).
6. If using a blender, put the top on but remove the little cap in the center (this will allow the steam to escape). Cover the cap hole with the clean dish towel. Turn the blender to the lowest speed and increase the speed as the soup purees. (If using a food processor, leave the plunger out while you puree the soup.)
7. As soon as the soup is pureed, pour it into another container. Repeat this same process until all the soup has been pureed. If you need to reheat the soup, pour it back into the pot and reheat over low.
8. Serve right away, or cover and refrigerate up to 3 days.

SAFETY ⚠ TIP
We are very serious about creating a way for the **steam to escape** when pureeing hot soup. There are four important steps:
1. Be sure to have the help of an adult.
2. Make sure the soup has cooled a bit.
3. Do not fill the blender all the way; fill it halfway at most.
4. Be sure you leave a way for steam to escape (see steps 5 and 6 above).

Fancy That!

To make any vegetable soup creamy: use ½ cup less broth and in its place, gradually stir in ½ cup plain yogurt, milk, or cream right before you serve the soup.

These are some of our favorite flavor combinations:

Asparagus Soup: Just before serving, add 1 teaspoon fresh tarragon or rosemary or 2 tablespoons fresh basil leaves. Garnish with Parmesan or feta cheese.

Butternut Squash or Carrots: When you add the onions, add 1 tablespoon finely minced fresh ginger, 1 tablespoon curry powder, and 1 apple, chopped, and/or replace ½ cup broth with orange or apple juice.

Cauliflower: When you add the onion, add 1 tablespoon finely minced fresh ginger and 1 tablespoon curry powder and/or 2 tablespoons chopped fresh cilantro and/or basil leaves.

Curried Anything: Add 1 tablespoon curry powder and ¼ cup plain yogurt or cream.

Cauliflower or Broccoli: Add ½ cup grated cheddar cheese when you puree the soup.

Corn: Add ½ cup fresh basil leaves when you puree the soup.

Tomato: Add ½ cup fresh basil leaves and ½ cup grated cheddar or Parmesan cheese when you puree the soup.

Perfect Pairings

Some flavors really complement particular vegetables—use your taste and creativity to come up with your own signature soups! Try adding any (but not all!) of the following.

Asparagus = chives, garlic, ginger, lemon zest and/or juice, mustard, plain yogurt or cream, Parmesan cheese, feta cheese

Broccoli = cheese, lemon zest and/or juice, plain yogurt or cream, thyme

Carrots = basil, chives, cilantro, fennel, ginger, tomatoes, plain yogurt or cream, curry powder

Cauliflower = cheese, chives, curry powder, garlic

Celery = curry powder, dill, lemon

Mushrooms = basil, garlic, lemon, mint, thyme, tomato

Butternut Squash/Pumpkin/Summer Squash = cinnamon, ginger, thyme

Zucchini = ginger, curry powder, plain yogurt or cream

Tomatoes = basil, chives, garlic, plain yogurt or cream

Winter Squash = apples, cinnamon, ginger, thyme, curry powder, plain yogurt or cream

Classic Red Gazpacho

Although gazpacho has come to mean almost any cold soup based on tomatoes and cucumbers, the original is from southern Spain. Like many traditional dishes, gazpacho varies depending on the cook. It's a little bit like a liquid salad. Consider all the ingredients as estimates: if you don't like bell peppers, add fewer or leave them out. Love your tomatoes chunky? Don't puree them. Whatever you do, try gazpacho, especially in the summer, when hot soup is less appealing and tomatoes and cucumbers are at their peak. Use the ripest tomatoes you can find.

ADULT NEEDED: YES • HANDS-ON TIME: 20 MINUTES • TOTAL TIME: 20 MINUTES • MAKES: ABOUT 6 CUPS

KITCHEN GEAR
Sharp knife (adult needed)
Cutting board
Measuring spoons
Measuring cup
Large bowl
Food processor or blender (adult needed)
Ladle

INGREDIENTS
2 English cucumbers, diced, or 3 conventional cucumbers, peeled, seeded, and diced
2 large tomatoes, cored and diced
1 small red or yellow onion, coarsely chopped
2 garlic cloves, peeled and minced or chopped
2 red bell peppers, cored, seeded, and coarsely chopped
2 tablespoons olive oil
3 tablespoons red wine vinegar
3 cups tomato juice
1 cup cold tap water
1 teaspoon cayenne pepper, if you like it spicy
1 teaspoon kosher salt
⅓ cup chopped fresh dill, cilantro, or basil leaves (if you like)
2 cups Croutons (page 85), for garnish (if you like)

INSTRUCTIONS
1. Put the cucumbers, tomatoes, onion, garlic, and peppers in the bowl and toss to combine.
2. Remove half the mixture and put it in the food processor fitted with a steel blade or in a blender.
3. Put the top on tightly and pulse 2 to 3 times until chopped and combined, but not pureed. Return to the bowl.
4. Add the oil, vinegar, tomato juice, water, cayenne, and salt and stir to combine.
5. Cover and refrigerate at least 2 hours and up to 3 days.
6. Just before serving, add the fresh herbs and Croutons (page 85), if you like.

Minestrone

Minestrone (min-eh-*strone*-ee) means "big soup" in Italian; just add bread and cheese and you have a whole meal. We consider it a vegetable soup with beans—the halfway point between vegetable soup and bean soup.

ADULT NEEDED: YES • HANDS-ON TIME: 20 MINUTES • TOTAL TIME: 2 HOURS • MAKES: ABOUT 12 CUPS

KITCHEN GEAR
Large heavy-bottomed pot
Measuring spoons
Sharp knife (adult needed)
Measuring cup
Cutting board
Can opener
Colander or strainer
Wooden spoon
Pot holders
Ladle

INGREDIENTS
1 tablespoon olive or vegetable oil
1 large onion, chopped
4 carrots, scrubbed or peeled, halved lengthwise and sliced
2 celery stalks, halved lengthwise and sliced
3–4 garlic cloves, peeled and minced or chopped
2 teaspoons dried basil
1 (16-ounce) can diced tomatoes, including liquid
10 cups low-sodium chicken, beef, or vegetable broth
½ bunch kale or ½ head green or Savoy cabbage (4–5 cups chopped)
⅓ cup brown rice or orzo
2 cups cooked or canned white or dark red kidney beans, drained and rinsed
Parmesan cheese, grated, for serving

INSTRUCTIONS
1. Put the pot on the stove and turn the heat to medium. When it is hot, carefully add the oil.
2. Add the onion, carrots, celery, garlic, and basil and cook, stirring, until the vegetables begin to soften, about 10 to15 minutes.
3. Add the tomatoes, broth, and kale and cook until it just starts to boil. Turn the heat down to low and cook 1 hour, without letting the soup boil again.
4. Add the rice and beans and cook until the rice is tender, about 40 minutes.
5. Serve right away, sprinkled with Parmesan cheese, or cover and refrigerate up to 3 days.

DID YOU KNOW?

Basil has some unusual connections to the scorpion! On the one hand, an African legend claims that basil protects against scorpions. On the other hand, seventeenth-century English botanist Nicholas Culpeper suggested that smelling basil could breed scorpions in the brain. (Um, not true, in case you're wondering.)

Bean Soups

Cooking dried beans can be much faster if you soak them overnight first. Alternatively, you can always use canned beans (just be sure to rinse them well with cold tap water).

Cooking Beans from Scratch

Beans are full of protein, fiber, vitamins, and deliciousness, and we like to use them in many of our recipes. It's fine to use beans from a can, but dried beans cooked from scratch are even tastier and less expensive. The method is the same for different kinds of beans, and all that changes is the cooking time.

ADULT NEEDED: YES • HANDS-ON TIME: 5 MINUTES • TOTAL TIME: 2–10 HOURS • MAKES: 4–5 CUPS COOKED BEANS

KITCHEN GEAR
Large pot with lid
Colander
Slotted spoon
Pot holder
Large container with lid

INGREDIENTS
1 pound dried beans (pinto, black, lima, navy, white, kidney, garbanzo, or any other kind of bean)

INSTRUCTIONS
1. Put the beans in the pot and sort through them, tossing out any shriveled beans, little stones, or twigs.
2. Pour cold tap water into the pot so the water comes up about 2 inches above the beans, then skim any stray bean skins or bits of stuff that float to the top. Depending on how much time you have, do one of these steps:
   - Cover the pot and leave the beans to soak either overnight or all day while you're at school, or
   - Put the pot on the stove and turn the heat to medium-high. When the water boils, turn off the heat, cover the pot, and leave the beans to soak for 1 hour.
3. Drain the soaked beans in the colander. Put them back in the pot and cover them with fresh cold tap water.
4. Put the pot on the stove and turn the heat to medium-high. When the water boils, turn the heat down to low, put the lid on the pot, and cook the beans until they are tender but not falling apart. This can take anywhere from ½ hour to 2 hours, depending on what kind of beans you have and how old they are. (Start testing the beans after they've been cooking for 30 minutes, and if they seem nearly done, then taste one in 15 minutes or so. If they don't seem quite done, taste in 30 minutes.)
5. Once the beans are cooked, set aside to cool.
6. Pour the beans into the colander and rinse with cold tap water.
7. Put the cooked beans in the container. Cover and refrigerate for up to 5 days.

Any-Many Bean Soup

Try to make this soup with an assortment of beans. In fact, the more the merrier. Although bean soups are generally better the second day, this one is great right away.

ADULT NEEDED: YES · HANDS-ON TIME: 30 MINUTES · TOTAL TIME: 2 HOURS · MAKES: 12 CUPS

KITCHEN GEAR
Sharp knife (adult needed)
Cutting board
Measuring spoons
Measuring cup
Large heavy-bottomed pot
Wooden spoon
Ladle

INGREDIENTS
2 teaspoons olive oil
1 onion, chopped
2 celery stalks, diced
5 carrots, scrubbed or peeled, and diced
2–3 garlic cloves, peeled and minced or chopped
2 bay leaves
6 cups assorted canned or cooked beans (kidney, black, white, garbanzo, or pinto), drained and rinsed
8 cups low-sodium chicken, beef, or vegetable broth
½ cup brown rice
1 tablespoon fresh lemon or lime juice
¼ cup chopped fresh basil or cilantro leaves

INSTRUCTIONS
1. Put the pot on the stove and turn the heat to medium. When it is hot, carefully add the oil.
2. Add the onion, celery, carrots, and garlic and cook until tender, 10 to 15 minutes. Stir occasionally.
3. Add the bay leaves, beans, and broth and bring to a boil. Turn the heat down to low and cook 1 ½ hours.
4. Add the rice and cook until tender, about 20 minutes.
5. Cover and refrigerate at least overnight and up to 3 days.
6. Just before serving, add the lemon or lime juice and basil or cilantro.

Why does soup get thicker as it cooks? As you heat soup, some of the water can turn to steam. This process is called evaporation. Unless the pot is covered, the steam can escape and there is less water in the remaining soup, making it thicker (which is generally what you want).

Black Bean Soup

Rich in flavor and soft in texture, black beans are perfect for soup. Black bean soup takes well to the flavors of cumin, chili, cilantro, and lime, but making it can be a project. It is time-consuming and tends to need lots of adjustments for flavor, but it is well worth it. It is best to start this soup the day before you want to serve it, or even two days before, to give the flavors time to blend and deepen. (But of course you can make and eat it the same day, if you like!)

ADULT NEEDED: YES · HANDS-ON TIME: 30 MINUTES · TOTAL TIME: 5 HOURS · MAKES: ABOUT 10 CUPS

KITCHEN GEAR
Colander
Large heavy-bottomed pot with lid
Measuring spoons
Sharp knife (adult needed)
Measuring cup
Wooden Spoon
Ladle

INGREDIENTS:
2 tablespoons olive oil
2 large onions, finely chopped
2 carrots, scrubbed or peeled, and chopped
2 celery stalks, chopped
4 garlic cloves, peeled and minced or chopped
1–2 teaspoons ground cumin
1–2 teaspoons chili powder
1 ½ teaspoons dried Greek oregano
½–1 teaspoon cayenne pepper
5–6 cups cooked or canned black beans, drained and rinsed
8 cups water or low-sodium chicken broth
2 tablespoons fresh lime juice (about 1 lime)
Chopped fresh cilantro leaves (if you like)
Plain yogurt or sour cream for garnish (if you like)

INSTRUCTIONS
1. Put the pot on the stove and turn the heat to medium. When it is hot, carefully add the oil.
2. Add the onions, carrots, celery, garlic, and spices and cook until tender, 10 to 15 minutes.
3. Add the beans and broth, raise the heat to high, and bring to a boil. Lower the heat to medium and cook, partially covered, for 2 hours, stirring occasionally.
4. After 2 hours, check to see if you need to add more broth. If the soup seems too thick and is starting to look like mud, add 1 to 2 more cups broth, raise the heat to high, and return to a boil.
5. Turn the heat down to low and cook, partially covered, for 2 hours, stirring occasionally.
6. Cover and refrigerate at least overnight and up to 3 days.
7. When ready to serve, put the soup in a pot on the stove and gently warm over low heat. Just before serving, add the lime juice, cilantro, and plain yogurt or sour cream, if you like.

White Bean Soup

White bean soup goes best with the flavor of a strong herb, like the rosemary we're using here.

ADULT NEEDED: YES · HANDS-ON TIME: 30 MINUTES · TOTAL TIME: 4 HOURS · MAKES: 8–10 CUPS

KITCHEN GEAR
Colander
Medium-sized bowl
Sharp knife (adult needed)
Measuring cup
Measuring spoons
Large heavy-bottomed pot with lid
Wooden spoon
Ladle
Container with lid

INGREDIENTS
4 cups cooked or canned white beans (such as navy, cannellini, or great Northern), drained and rinsed
2 garlic cloves, peeled and minced or chopped
1 onion, coarsely chopped
2 celery stalks, halved lengthwise and sliced
2 carrots, scrubbed or peeled, and cut into quarters lengthwise and sliced
1 large potato, scrubbed and cubed (about 1 ½ cups)
2 teaspoons dried rosemary, or 2 tablespoons chopped fresh rosemary, plus extra for garnish (if you like)
8 cups low-sodium chicken broth
1 (16-ounce) can diced tomatoes
1 tablespoon fresh lemon juice or red wine vinegar
¼ cup chopped fresh Italian flat-leaf parsley leaves

INSTRUCTIONS
1. Put the pot on the stove, add the beans, garlic, onion, celery, carrots, potato, rosemary, and broth, and turn the heat to high.
2. When the mixture comes to a boil, turn the heat down to low and cook, partially covered, until the beans have fallen apart, about 2 hours, stirring occasionally.
3. Add the tomatoes and continue to cook, partially covered, until the soup begins to thicken, about ½ hour, stirring occasionally.
4. Cover and refrigerate at least overnight and up to 3 days.
5. When ready to serve, put the soup in a pot on the stove and gently warm over low heat. Just before serving, add the lemon juice and parsley, and fresh rosemary, if you like.

Be Creative
You can halve the amount of white beans and make this a brothier soup.

Split Pea Soup

Split pea soup is usually made with ham, and while there is nothing wrong with that, we wanted to try a lighter version that was still rich tasting. The tart, bright lemon goes perfectly with the thick, creamy peas.

ADULT NEEDED: YES • ACTIVE TIME: 30 MINUTES • TOTAL TIME: 3 ½ HOURS • MAKES: 10 CUPS

KITCHEN GEAR
Measuring spoons
Sharp knife (adult needed)
Colander
Measuring cup
Large heavy-bottomed pot with lid
Wooden spoon
Ladle

INGREDIENTS
2 teaspoons olive, canola, or vegetable oil
1 onion, finely chopped
½ pound carrots, scrubbed or peeled, cut into quarters lengthwise and sliced
1 teaspoon dried tarragon, or 1 tablespoon chopped fresh tarragon leaves
1 pound split peas, rinsed in the colander and picked over (page 65)
10 cups low-sodium chicken or vegetable broth
2 tablespoons fresh lemon juice

INSTRUCTIONS
1. Put the pot on the stove and turn the heat to medium. When it is hot, carefully add the oil.
2. Add the onion and cook until tender, about 10 to 15 minutes.
3. Add the carrots, tarragon, split peas, and broth.
4. Raise the heat to high and bring to a boil. Turn the heat down to low and cook, partially covered, until the peas have fallen apart, about 2 hours, stirring occasionally. Using the spoon carefully skim off the foam that forms. Add the lemon juice.
5. Serve right away, or cover and refrigerate up to 3 days.

Note: If you serve this soup on the following day, you will need to add more broth, as the soup is guaranteed to thicken overnight.

Beans and lentils pack almost as much protein as chicken or fish, and they have a lot more healthy fiber and other vitamins and minerals that are great for growing bodies.

Lentil Soup

Lentils are shaped like flying saucers, and they come in lots of different colors. Regular lentils can be green or brown, and there are small marbled-green French lentils, black Beluga lentils, and "red" lentils that are actually orange. For this soup, use any kind but the red ones (they break down too much and make the soup porridgy). Lentils are called "pulses" and are a cousin to the bean. We treat them differently from most dried beans because they don't need to be soaked before you cook them.

ADULT NEEDED: YES • HANDS-ON TIME: 15 MINUTES • TOTAL TIME: 3–4 ¼ HOURS • MAKES: 10–12 CUPS

KITCHEN GEAR
Measuring cup
Measuring spoons
Colander or strainer
Large heavy-bottomed pot
Cutting board
Sharp knife (adult needed)
Vegetable peeler
Wooden spoon
Ladle

INGREDIENTS
1　cup lentils, rinsed in the colander and picked over (page 65)
4　scallions, greens and whites, sliced
1　carrot, scrubbed or peeled, and sliced
2　celery stalks, including leaves, sliced
½　teaspoon dried oregano
¼　cup raw barley or brown rice
12 cups low-sodium chicken, beef, or vegetable broth
1 (16-ounce) can whole peeled tomatoes, coarsely chopped
Kosher salt and black pepper
Lemon quarters
1　tablespoon chopped fresh basil, parsley, or cilantro leaves

INSTRUCTIONS
1. Put the pot on the stove, add the lentils, scallions, carrot, celery, oregano, barley or rice, and broth into the pot, and turn the heat to high.
2. When it comes to a boil, turn the heat down to low and cook, uncovered, until the soup has thickened and the volume in the pot is about ¼ less full than when you started, about 2 hours. Stir occasionally to make sure it's not sticking to the bottom.
3. Add the tomatoes and continue to cook 1 to 2 more hours, stirring occasionally.
4. Add salt and pepper to taste. Serve right away with the lemon quarters and basil, parsley, or cilantro, or cover and refrigerate up to 3 days.

Why do you add the tomatoes so late? If you add the tomatoes too early, the lentils won't soften fast enough. But adding them later makes the liquid more acidic and causes the lentils to hold their shape so they don't totally fall apart.

Breads

"Quick bread" doesn't necessarily mean your bread will be out of the oven in a jiffy—usually it just refers to any kind of bread you make without yeast. Still, you'll be able to make any of these in the time it takes your soup to cook, and it's very satisfying to pull a pan of rolls or biscuits or cornbread out of the oven. Make any of these breads to pair with any of these soups and you have dinner. Make the soup the day before and you have the ultimate fast food.

Cornbread

It's classic to serve cornbread with chili, but it's great alongside other soups, too. Plus, because you mix the batter briefly and pour it directly into the pan, it's great for times when you don't want to fuss with shaping dough.

ADULT NEEDED: YES • HANDS-ON TIME: 20 MINUTES • TOTAL TIME: 1 HOUR AND 15 MINUTES • MAKES: 12 SQUARES

KITCHEN GEAR
8-inch square baking pan
Measuring cup
Measuring spoons
Large mixing bowl
Small mixing bowl
Fork or whisk
Large spoon

INGREDIENTS
¼ cup olive, canola, or vegetable oil, plus 1 teaspoon
1 cup yellow cornmeal
1 ½ cups all-purpose flour
2 teaspoons baking powder
1 teaspoon kosher salt
2 large eggs, lightly beaten
1 ½ cups plain yogurt or buttermilk
¼ cup real maple syrup or honey

INSTRUCTIONS
1. Turn the oven on and set it to 350 degrees. Using your clean hand or a paper towel, lightly coat the pan with 1 teaspoon oil.
2. Put the cornmeal, flour, baking powder, salt, and real maple syrup or honey in the large mixing bowl.
3. Put the eggs, yogurt or buttermilk, and ¼ cup oil in the small mixing bowl and mix well. Add the egg mixture to the flour mixture and stir until just combined (don't worry about it being smooth).
4. Spoon the batter into the prepared pan and carefully put the pan in the oven. Bake until the top is golden brown, 45 to 55 minutes. Cut into 12 squares and serve warm or at room temperature.

Multigrain Rolls

These rolls use lots of interesting grains that add lots of great flavor and texture.

ADULT NEEDED: YES • HANDS-ON TIME: 20 MINUTES • TOTAL TIME: 40 MINUTES • MAKES: 24 ROLLS

KITCHEN GEAR
Baking sheet
Parchment paper
Measuring cup
Measuring spoons
Food processor (adult needed)
Large mixing bowl
Rubber spatula
Sharp knife (adult needed)
Pastry brush

INGREDIENTS
2 cups all-purpose flour
1 cup whole-wheat or Graham flour
½ cup yellow cornmeal
¼ cup toasted wheat germ
¼ cup ground flaxseed
1 tablespoon baking powder
2 teaspoons kosher salt
2 teaspoons sugar
1 teaspoon baking soda
1 ½ sticks unsalted butter, chilled or frozen, cut into thin slices
2 large eggs
1 ½ cups plain yogurt
1 cup currants or raisins (if you like)
1 large egg yolk, beaten

Super Soda! Baking soda is really similar to baking powder. In fact, baking powder contains baking soda, but it needs to be mixed with specific ingredients to release gas.

Power Powder! Baking powder releases carbon dioxide (that's the gas we breathe out) after it has been mixed with water. The gas released creates little air bubbles in the biscuits, making them light and fluffy instead of heavy and dense.

INSTRUCTIONS
1. Turn the oven on and set it to 375 degrees. Line a baking sheet with parchment paper.
2. Put the flours, cornmeal, wheat germ, flaxseed, baking powder, salt, sugar, and baking soda in the bowl of the food processor fitted with a steel blade and process until combined. While the machine is running, add the butter a few slices at a time through the feeding tube at the top, and process until the mixture looks like cornmeal.
3. Put the eggs and yogurt in the bowl and mix well. Add the flour mixture and currants or raisins, if you like, and mix with your clean hands until combined.
4. Divide into 24 balls. Put the balls on the prepared baking sheet and, using your palm, flatten each ball down a bit. Using the tip of the knife, make an X in the tops and then brush with the egg yolk.
5. Put the baking sheet in the oven and bake until the top of the roll is golden brown and the bottom of the roll sounds hollow when tapped, about 20 minutes. Repeat with the remaining dough. Serve warm.

Crazy-Good Buttermilk Biscuits

These biscuits bake up puffy, flaky, and wonderful. By Catherine Newman

ADULT NEEDED: YES · HANDS-ON TIME: 30 MINUTES · TOTAL TIME: 45 MINUTES · MAKES: 12 (2-INCH) BISCUITS

KITCHEN GEAR
Large baking sheet
Measuring cup
Measuring spoons
Large bowl
Fork
Cutting board
Round cookie cutter, biscuit cutter, or
    drinking glass
Pot holder

INGREDIENTS
1   cup all-purpose flour
1   cup whole-wheat flour
2   teaspoons baking powder
½   teaspoon baking soda
½   teaspoon kosher salt
6   tablespoons (¾ stick) unsalted butter,
    cut into small pieces
1   cup buttermilk or plain yogurt

INSTRUCTIONS
1. Turn the oven on and set it to 450 degrees. Using your clean hand or a paper towel, lightly coat the baking sheet with canola or vegetable oil.
2. Put the flours, baking powder, baking soda, and salt in the bowl and mix well.
3. Put the butter pieces in the bowl and toss them around gently to coat them with the flour mixture. Use your fingertips to rub the butter into the dry ingredients: you'll be lifting handfuls of the mixture slightly above the bowl, then gently letting it fall through your fingertips as you rub it lightly together. Eventually, you'll have a bowl full of lumpy sandlike stuff, which is what you want.
4. Add the buttermilk or yogurt and, using the fork, stir until the mixture is evenly moistened.
5. Sprinkle a little flour on a clean counter or cutting board and dump the dough lumps onto it, and gently press it all together with your clean hands. Pat the dough into a circle that's about ¾ inch thick. Press the cookie cutter, biscuit cutter, or drinking glass down into the dough to cut your biscuits, laying them on the baking sheet as you go.
6. When you've cut as many biscuits as you can, pat together another circle with the dough scraps, then cut out the rest of the biscuits.
7. Carefully put the baking sheet in the oven and bake until golden brown, about 12 to 15 minutes.
8. Use the pot holder to remove the baking sheet from the oven. Serve warm.

DID YOU KNOW?

Originally, buttermilk was the liquid left behind after making butter. Now, buttermilk is a processed and cultured version of milk. It is thick and yogurty.

Salads

A green salad is like a favorite pair of jeans: it goes with everything and there's always something just right about it.

Plus, it's one of the best ways we know to make sure you're getting a big serving of fresh vegetables. A salad can be as simple as a giant bowl of greens, or as complicated as a mosaic of color and texture. And what really makes a salad special? The dressing, of course. Which is why this chapter might seem a little bit backward: we're going to teach you to make dressing first, assuming that if you can make great dressing, then the salad's in the bag. Maybe even literally: bagged salad greens make life so easy these days for all us salad lovers. If you've got a bag of greens and a jar of homemade dressing in the fridge, you're less than a minute away from eating a salad. Unless you want to get fancy—and we'll show you how to do that, too, with our colorful power-salad ingredients that add color and crunch.

Be Creative

A green salad is a great way to turn a bowl of soup or a sandwich into a complete meal. Or, go the other way and turn salad itself into the main dish by adding any or all of the following protein-rich additions:

- Grilled (or leftover) chicken, salmon, shrimp, or steak
- Canned or fresh tuna, sardines, or anchovies
- Tofu (raw, baked, or grilled)
- Hard-cooked eggs, sliced or cut into quarters

- Crumbled or grated cheese
- Toasted nuts
- Cooked or canned beans, including edamame, black beans, kidney beans, white beans, pinto beans, and chickpeas

Salad Dressings

Making your own salad dressing is so easy, so quick, and so yummy, we don't really understand why anyone would buy it ready-made from a store. Make a few of these easy dressings to have on hand, and having salad every night will be a breeze. Just be sure to have a ready supply of bottles or jars with tight-fitting lids (canning jars are perfect).

Basic Dressing Method

ADULT NEEDED: YES (WHEN KNIFE USED) • HANDS-ON TIME: 20 MINUTES • TOTAL TIME: 20 MINUTES • MAKES: ABOUT 1 CUP

All our dressings use the same kitchen gear and follow the same set of instructions.
An adult will be needed when you use a sharp knife or blender or food processor.

KITCHEN GEAR
Cutting board
Sharp knife (adult needed)
Measuring cup
Measuring spoons
Glass jar with lid or small bowl
Fork or whisk

INSTRUCTIONS
1. Put all the ingredients in a jar, put the lid on tightly, and shake, shake, shake.
2. Or put all the ingredients in a bowl and whisk, whisk, whisk.

Why do you have to mix the ingredients so quickly and completely? Most salad dressings are emulsions, which means a mixture of ingredients that don't usually blend together (like that expression "oil and water don't mix").

When you try salad dressing right from the jar it should be a little too strong. Once it gets on salad greens the flavor will be less intense. Either way, taste it before you add it to the greens and adjust as you like: Does it need more salt? More pepper? More lemon juice? If so, add and taste again.

Caesar Dressing

Caesar salad—a mix of romaine lettuce, croutons, Parmesan cheese, and a richly flavored dressing—is offered at many restaurants. But most of the salads you order won't be nearly as fresh tasting and delicious as the one you make yourself. After all, most restaurants make their dressing in big vats and often don't use the same ingredients in the proportions that make this recipe really great. Try this yourself and don't leave out the anchovies, even if you think you don't like them! Most people never even know they're in there—they just add a little salty-rich flavor you can't quite put your finger on.

INGREDIENTS
- 4 garlic cloves, peeled and minced or chopped
- 2–3 anchovies, minced
- ½ teaspoon Dijon mustard
- ½ cup fresh lemon juice (about 2 lemons)
- ½ cup olive oil
- ¼–½ cup grated Parmesan cheese

DID YOU KNOW?

Anchovies are tiny fish, typically under four inches long. They're usually preserved in salt and instead of being eaten the way you would a piece of salmon, they're used as a condiment, which is something added to food to give it more flavor.

By the numbers: One serving of anchovies contains 597 milligrams (a lot) of omega-3, a nutrient that is called a "fatty acid," which helps keep your body and brain healthy.

Oregano-Garlic Vinaigrette

Garlic keeps your heart and immune system healthy. Some people think garlic is stinky, but we don't: it adds a great flavor and fragrance to this dressing.

INGREDIENTS
¾ cup olive oil

½ cup red wine vinegar

1–2 garlic cloves, peeled and minced or chopped

1 teaspoon dried oregano

¼ teaspoon kosher salt

⅛ teaspoon black pepper

Lemony Vinaigrette

The word "vinaigrette" usually refers to an emulsion of oil and vinegar, but you can still use the term when lemon juice stands in for the vinegar (both are tart and acidic). We love this dressing drizzled on greens, cooked grains like couscous and pasta, or on chicken and salmon.

INGREDIENTS
¾ cup olive oil

6 tablespoons fresh lemon juice or red wine vinegar

1 teaspoon Dijon mustard

½ teaspoon water

¼ teaspoon kosher salt

⅛ teaspoon black pepper

DID YOU KNOW? The phrase "Can't cut the mustard" means that a thing or person can't live up to a challenge.

Balsamic Vinaigrette

This is an all-purpose, slightly sweet vinaigrette that's great drizzled on just about all greens, vegetables, and cold tuna or chicken. You can also use it for marinating chicken and steak.

INGREDIENTS
¾ cup olive oil

6 tablespoons balsamic vinegar

2 garlic cloves, peeled and minced or chopped

1 teaspoon Dijon mustard

¼ teaspoon kosher salt

⅛ teaspoon black pepper

What is balsamic vinegar? Like wine vinegar, it's made from fermented grapes, but it has a sweeter flavor and a very dark color. Traditional balsamic vinegar is aged more than 12 years and requires 70 pounds (the average weight of a Labrador retriever) of grapes to produce one single cup of vinegar! (Most of the balsamic vinegar you see at the store is made more quickly.)

Avocado Dressing

Avocadoes are naturally rich in good-for-you fats, which means that this creamy, delicious dressing doesn't need any added oil! It's great on sliced tomatoes and green salads.

INGREDIENTS
1 ripe avocado, peeled, pitted, and mashed
1 cup buttermilk
¼ cup fresh lemon juice
2 garlic cloves, peeled and minced or chopped
¼ teaspoon kosher salt
⅛ teaspoon black pepper

How do you know when an avocado is ripe? When you gently press the stem end, an avocado should feel just a little soft—not too hard (which means it's unripe) and not too soft (which means it's overripe). If your avocadoes are hard when you get them home from the store, don't refrigerate them; put them in a brown paper bag to ripen. This traps ethylene, the gas the avocadoes produce, and helps them ripen faster. To really speed things along, put an unpeeled banana in the bag with them! The banana makes extra ethylene. Once the avocadoes are ripe, store them in the fridge.

Pesto Dressing

Deeply flavorful, but not quite as intense as pesto, this is a wonderful dressing to pair with tomatoes.

INGREDIENTS
½ cup olive oil
¼ cup red or white wine vinegar
3 tablespoons chopped fresh basil leaves
1 garlic clove, peeled and minced or chopped
1 tablespoon toasted pine nuts, walnuts, or almonds, if you like, chopped
1 tablespoon grated Parmesan cheese
⅛ teaspoon kosher salt
⅛ teaspoon black pepper

DID YOU KNOW?

Vinegar is made through a process called "fermentation." A particular type of bacteria, called an acetobacter, turns alcohol, such as wine or hard cider, into acetic acid. The final liquid doesn't have any alcohol left in it, and tastes sour because of the acid.

Soy Salad Dressing

Have you ever heard the term *umami*? It's a Japanese word that describes food that tastes kind of salty and makes you crave more—a flavor you can't put your finger on, but is insanely delicious! This salad dressing is totally *umami*! Pour it on a green salad, use it to marinate tofu, or stir it into a heap of shredded cabbage for a new kind of coleslaw.

INGREDIENTS
⅔ cup unseasoned rice vinegar or fresh lime juice
⅓ cup canola or vegetable oil
1 tablespoon low-sodium soy sauce

What is rice vinegar? Rice vinegar is made from fermented rice, instead of the grapes used in balsamic or wine vinegar or the apples used in cider vinegar.

Creamy Blue Cheese Dressing

We love this best on hearty greens like romaine or iceberg lettuce, or with cut-up vegetables (sometimes called crudités).

INGREDIENTS
¾ cup crumbled blue cheese

½ cup buttermilk

¼ cup whole-milk yogurt, taken from the creamy top, if possible

2 teaspoons fresh lemon juice

⅛ teaspoon kosher salt

⅛ teaspoon black pepper

Why is blue cheese blue? The blue color comes from a type of mold. It is completely edible and is related to the same organism that produces the antibiotic penicillin.

Ranch Dressing

Everybody loves ranch dressing, but our version not only tastes fresher than bottled, it's healthier and more delicious. Serve it as a salad dressing or as a dip with carrots, cucumbers, or celery.

INGREDIENTS
½ cup plain Greek yogurt

2 tablespoons buttermilk or low-fat or whole milk

2 tablespoons olive oil

1 tablespoon white vinegar

1 tablespoon finely chopped fresh dill or parsley leaves or chives

½ teaspoon mustard (any kind is fine)

1 teaspoon finely chopped onion or ½ teaspoon onion powder

½ teaspoon finely chopped garlic or ¼ teaspoon garlic powder

⅛ teaspoon kosher salt

⅛ teaspoon black pepper

Croutons

You know how we feel about bottled salad dressing—*why would anyone buy it?* We feel even more that way about croutons! Make your own fresh, crunchy, delicious croutons, and leave the bagged kind in the dust (which is what they kind of taste like). Plus, croutons are a great way to use up stale bread.

ADULT NEEDED: YES • HANDS-ON TIME: 10 MINUTES • TOTAL TIME: 30 MINUTES • MAKES: 4–5 CUPS

KITCHEN GEAR
Sharp knife (adult needed)

Large bowl

Measuring cup

Measuring spoons

Baking sheet

Pot holders

INGREDIENTS
4–5 cups ½-inch cubes of day-old bread (any kind is fine)

2 tablespoons olive, canola, or vegetable oil

1–2 garlic cloves, peeled and minced or chopped

1 teaspoon kosher salt

1 tablespoon grated Parmesan, Romano, or Asiago cheese (if you like)

INSTRUCTIONS
1. Turn the oven on and set it to 350 degrees.
2. Put the bread, oil, garlic, salt, and cheese, if you like, in the bowl and toss to combine.
3. Dump the bread onto the baking sheet and spread the cubes out evenly.
4. Carefully put the baking sheet in the oven and bake until just golden, 15 to 20 minutes. Set aside to cool completely.
5. Serve right away, or put in a zipper-lock bag and freeze up to 2 weeks.

The Salad Itself

If you can make salad dressing, you can make an amazing salad. Don't just think about iceberg and romaine lettuce: Be brave! Be daring! There are tons of salad greens to choose from. Below we show you a lot of greens and try to explain what they taste like. And on the next page, we offer a list of other fresh, delicious ingredients you might consider adding to your salad. The best salads include all kinds of flavors and textures, including salty, sweet, crunchy, and creamy. Just open your mind before you open your mouth!

Greens:

- **Arugula:** also called "rocket"; peppery and spicy
- **Belgian endive:** bitter and crunchy; great paired with strong, creamy cheeses
- **Bibb lettuce:** mild and sweet
- **Boston lettuce:** buttery, very soft leaves
- **Chervil:** a licoricey herb
- **Chicory (curly endive):** has a nice bite but can be slightly bitter to some
- **Cress:** hot and peppery
- **Dandelion greens:** nice and bitter; warm the dressing to mellow out the bitterness
- **Endive:** sweet, bitter, and crunchy
- **Frisée:** slightly sweet, slightly bitter; good paired with nuts and cheese
- **Green oak-leaf lettuce:** mild and slightly grassy

- **Green chard:** spinachlike; use baby leaves for salad
- **Iceberg lettuce:** crisp, mild, and delicious with Creamy Blue Cheese Dressing (page 85)
- **Mâche (also called lambs lettuce or corn salad):** delicate flavor, best served alone
- **Mizuna:** mustardy Japanese green
- **Mustard greens:** crunchy, slightly bitter and cabbagey
- **Radicchio:** beautiful deep red color; bitter and slightly peppery
- **Red chard (and beet greens):** slightly sweet and grassy; use baby leaves in salad
- **Red oak-leaf lettuce:** mild and slightly nutty
- **Romaine lettuce:** very crunchy, slightly sweet, slightly bitter
- **Watercress:** peppery, spicy, great with citrus fruit

Other stuff to add to salads

- Fresh fruit, including grapes, berries, sliced or diced apples, pears, peaches, nectarines, kiwi, and mango, and sectioned tangerines, oranges, grapefruit, and clementines
- Dried fruit, including apricots, raisins, currants, cherries, figs, and dates
- Cooked and cooled vegetables, such as green beans, peas, asparagus, corn, cauliflower, and broccoli
- Fresh herbs, such as cilantro, basil, parsley, dill, chives, or mint
- Cooked, cooled, and sliced potatoes
- Tomatoes, any kind: cherry, beefsteak, plum, yellow
- Raw vegetables such as sliced or diced cucumbers, mushrooms, carrots, bell peppers, jicama, radishes, celery, and fennel
- Grated raw carrots or beets
- Sprouts, especially nice peppery ones like broccoli or radish sprouts
- Pickled beets
- Roasted peppers
- Olives, black or green
- Thinly sliced onions, especially sweet ones like Bermuda, Walla Walla, or Vidalia
- Cheeses, almost any crumbled or grated, including feta, Parmesan, cheddar, blue, Brie, and goat
- Canned or marinated artichoke hearts
- Grilled or leftover chicken, beef, shrimp, tofu
- Cooked beans, including black, white, garbanzo, red kidney, and pinto
- Toasted nuts or seeds

Ideas for salad combinations

Eat alone or add to greens:

- Barley with sliced carrots, celery, and mushrooms
- Diced or sliced tomatoes, fresh basil leaves, and crumbled feta cheese
- Farro, chickpeas, diced tomatoes, crumbled feta cheese, and fresh mint leaves
- Brown rice, shredded chicken, shredded cabbage, fresh cilantro, toasted sesame seeds
- Diced avocado and grapefruit
- Diced mango, avocado, and black beans
- Corn and black beans
- Sliced or diced cucumber, peach, radish, and toasted walnuts
- Diced celery, oranges, and feta cheese
- Strawberry, chopped asparagus, and avocado
- Cheddar cubes, diced apple, celery, and toasted walnuts
- Diced cucumber, radishes, and sesame seeds
- Grapes, toasted almonds, and shredded chicken
- Brown rice, shaved carrots, cucumbers, radishes celery, onion, peas, and fresh parsley

How to Use a Salad Spinner

1. Remove the strainer (the plastic part in the center) from the salad spinner.
2. Tear or cut up your lettuce or other greens and dump them in the strainer.
3. Run cold tap water over the greens and shake them around until all the dirt is off.
4. Put the strainer back in the spinner and put the lid on.
5. Hold the spinner steady with one hand and press down on the top part or pull the ripcord with your other hand. Keep spinning fast for about 15 seconds.
6. Test for dryness and then repeat if needed.

Dinner

You've probably heard how important it is for families to share a meal together. It's not just something parents say— researchers have demonstrated that it has all kinds of real benefits.

Plus, sharing a meal, particularly at the end of the day, just feels right: it's a great time to nourish ourselves and each other, a time to reconnect and relax. It also may be the only time you have to cook, so this chapter might be of special interest to you if you're hoping to make a meal for—or with—your family.

We encourage you to open your mind about dinner: pair any soup and salad from this book and you have a solid dinner. Or make a yummy dip, cut up a platter of vegetables, and put out some whole-grain bread. Sandwiches, egg dishes, bread and cheese with some oven-roasted vegetables—all of these are dinner in our book.

Still, if you're looking for the classics, here they are: our favorite chicken dishes, burgers, tofu recipes, pastas, and the vegetables to go with them—just a few of each with lots of easy variations, so you can figure out what you like and how you like to make them. You'll feel proud to cook dinner for your family. And your family will feel lucky for the occasion to celebrate: everybody together, with good food on the table.

Not Just Food

There are so many details that can make even a weeknight meal feel special.

- **Set the table nicely.** Is there a tablecloth that's okay to use? (If not, get a roll of white or craft paper and make one). If your family has a special set of dishes or glasses, ask your adult if you can use them. You're cooking, and it's nice to treat it like a special occasion.

- **Light candles.** No, you're not at a fancy restaurant, but it's so easy to do, and candlelight makes every meal feel luxurious. (Remember, of course, to ask your adult.)

- **Make a no-tech rule for dinnertime.** Some families keep a basket where everyone, including guests, can deposit their phones and devices before sitting down to eat.

- **Start a conversation.** Try writing questions on slips of paper and keeping them in a jar. At each meal, someone can pull out a slip and everyone can take turns sharing their answers. Open-ended (rather than yes/no) questions are best for this: *If you could change one thing about the world, what would it be? If you could have dinner with any person, living or dead, who would you choose and why?*

A Few Great Chicken Recipes

People will tell you all the crazy things they've tried that taste just like chicken: rattlesnake, wild mushrooms, you name it. But you know what tastes just like chicken? Chicken! Well, it tastes like chicken, and also like whatever you season it with: spices, herbs, sauces, and even just the roasting heat of a hot oven. It's readily available, easily adaptable, a good source of protein—and almost everybody likes it.

Whole Roasted Chicken

A roasted chicken is one of those easy but impressive meals: the oven does all the work, but when you bring a beautifully golden chicken to the table on a platter, you'll feel like you did something amazing. Plus, you can use leftovers for sandwiches, wraps, quesadillas, and salads—or the Chicken Stew on page 99!

ADULT NEEDED: YES • HANDS-ON TIME: 20 MINUTES • TOTAL TIME: 1 ¾ HOURS • MAKES: 4–6 SERVINGS

KITCHEN GEAR
Roasting rack
Roasting pan
Measuring spoons
Sharp knife (adult needed)
Cutting board
Pot holders
Instant-read meat thermometer (if you have one)

INGREDIENTS
1 whole roaster chicken, about 3–5 pounds
1–1 ½ teaspoons kosher salt
¼ teaspoon black pepper
1 lemon, cut into quarters

INSTRUCTIONS
1. Turn the oven on and set it to 450 degrees.
2. Take the chicken out of its package and remove and throw away the giblets and neck from the chicken cavity (yes, this can be kind of gross).
3. Put the chicken on the roasting rack and rub it with the salt and pepper. Put the lemon quarters in the cavities.
4. Put the roasting rack in the pan and carefully move it to the oven. (Ask your adult for help.)
5. Roast the chicken for 1 hour and 10 minutes. Ask your adult to help move the roasting pan to the top of the stove and close the oven door. If you are using a thermometer, insert it deep into the inner thigh: the chicken is done when the internal temperature reaches 160 degrees. If you do not have a thermometer, you can tell when the chicken is done with one of these tests: poke the breast with a knife and look at the juice that runs out—it should be clear (not pink)—or ask your adult to wiggle the leg, which should move easily. If it's not done, put it back in the oven and test it again after 15 minutes. (As you get more and more experienced, your adult may let you take on some of the more expert jobs.)
6. Let the chicken rest on a cutting board for 15 to 20 minutes before asking your adult to carve it.

SAFETY ! TIP
Wash your hands with soap and water after you touch raw chicken.

Be Creative

Hungarian: Sprinkle the chicken with 2 teaspoons Hungarian paprika before roasting.

Italian: Add 1 sprig fresh rosemary and 2 chopped garlic cloves to the cavity before roasting.

Fruity: Instead of filling the cavity with a lemon, use a cut-up orange, apple, or onion.

Herby: Add ¼ cup fresh herbs (thyme, rosemary, parsley, marjoram, and/or sage) to the cavity before roasting.

Roasted Chicken (Pieces)

To "chicken out" means to be scared—but this easy, hearty meal is nothing to be afraid of! The nice thing about cooking chicken parts is that you can make sure to get just what everyone in your family likes.

ADULT NEEDED: YES • HANDS-ON TIME: 20 MINUTES • TOTAL TIME: 1 HOUR AND 20 MINUTES • MAKES: 4 SERVINGS

KITCHEN GEAR
Large rimmed baking sheet
Sharp knife (adult needed)
Cutting board
Measuring spoons
Serving spoon
Large plate

INGREDIENTS
4 bone-in, skin-on chicken breasts or large thighs or legs or a combination (as long as there is enough for everyone), trimmed of fat
1 red onion, sliced
2 small seedless oranges, peeled and separated into sections
½ teaspoon kosher salt
½ teaspoon black pepper
1 lemon, cut into quarters

INSTRUCTIONS
1. Turn the oven on and set it to 450 degrees.
2. Put the chicken, onion, and oranges on a baking sheet in one layer. Be sure nothing overlaps with anything else. Sprinkle the chicken with the salt and pepper.
3. Put the baking sheet in the oven and cook until the chicken is browned on top and, for breasts, white inside (no longer pink—you'll need to cut into a piece with a sharp knife) and the onions and fruit have softened and darkened, 45 minutes to 1 hour.
4. Move the chicken to a large plate. Squeeze the lemon juice over the fruit and onions and then top the chicken with the roasted fruit mixture. Serve right away.

Be Creative
Substitute apples, cored and cut into 8 sections, for the oranges.

Why do you need to cook the chicken in one layer? To keep the chicken from steaming rather than roasting. By keeping the food in one layer, steam can more easily leave it and everything can have contact with the hot pan, which helps brown it.

How to Trim the Fat off a Skin-on Piece of Chicken

Using clean hands, lay the chicken flat, skin-side up, on a clean cutting board. Push the chicken down a bit so the excess fat is on the cutting board (the excess is the part that isn't right on top of the chicken). Now, using clean kitchen scissors or a sharp knife (ask your adult for help), cut off and throw away the excess.

Not Your Grandma's Fried Chicken

Oven-fried chicken is way better than pan-fried (don't tell Grandma). It's so much easier to make, it's a lot better for you, and it doesn't smoke up the kitchen!

ADULT NEEDED: YES · HANDS-ON TIME: 30 MINUTES · TOTAL TIME: 1 ½ HOURS · MAKES: 4 SERVINGS

KITCHEN GEAR
Baking sheet
Large bowl
Mixing spoon or whisk
Large plate
Large skillet
Heatproof spatula or tongs

INGREDIENTS
2 tablespoons olive, canola, or vegetable oil
1 cup fine bread crumbs or Panko
½ cup whole-wheat flour
1 teaspoon kosher salt
½ teaspoon black pepper
¼ teaspoon cayenne pepper, if you like it spicy
2 large eggs
1 tablespoon Dijon mustard
1 teaspoon dried thyme
6 boneless, skinless chicken thighs or breasts, trimmed of fat
1 lemon, cut into quarters

INSTRUCTIONS
1. Using your clean hands or a paper towel, lightly coat the baking sheet with oil.
2. Put the bread crumbs, flour, salt and pepper, and cayenne (if you like it spicy) on the plate. Mix well.
3. Crack the eggs and put them into the bowl. Add the mustard and thyme and mix well. Add the chicken pieces and swish them around until they are well coated with the egg mixture.
4. Remove the chicken pieces, one at a time, from the egg mixture and let any extra egg mixture drip off.
5. Dip the chicken pieces, one at a time, in the bread crumb mixture, rolling them and pressing down to coat each side (don't worry if you don't cover it completely).
6. Shake off any extra coating, then put the chicken pieces on the baking sheet. Cover and refrigerate at least 30 minutes and up to 2 hours. This step is very important in order to make the coating stick.
7. Turn the oven on and set it to 400 degrees.
8. Carefully put the baking sheet in the oven and bake for 15 minutes. Using a spatula or tongs, turn the chicken pieces over and bake until golden brown, 15 to 20 more minutes. Serve right away, with a lemon quarter on each plate.

Do I really need to refrigerate the chicken after I bread it? Yes, yes, yes! The refrigeration step dries out the surface of the chicken pieces, which helps to speed up the browning process and gives you a nice crunchy crust.

Be Creative
Chicken Fingers: Use chicken tenders instead of thighs or breasts.
Herby Chicken: Double the amount of thyme or substitute dried tarragon, oregano, or basil for the thyme.
Corny Chicken: Substitute crushed cornflakes for the bread crumbs.
Cheesy Chicken: Add 2 tablespoons shredded Parmesan cheese to the bread crumbs.
Zesty Chicken: Add 2 teaspoons lemon or orange zest to the bread crumbs.
Nutty Chicken: Substitute finely chopped pecans or almonds for ½ cup bread crumbs.

DID YOU KNOW?

Panko is a Japanese-style bread crumb that is made from bread without crusts. You can buy it ready made at most grocery or specialty stores.

Chicken Stew Five Ways
(Classic, Jamaican, Indian, French, and Greek)

One of the greatest, most fun things about cooking is that once you learn a basic recipe or technique, you can adapt it to make dishes just the way you like them. Here we're showing you how one simple recipe for a hearty chicken stew can go in different directions, depending on the seasoning you use. Serve this stew over pasta, brown rice, barley, or Israeli couscous.

ADULT NEEDED: YES • HANDS-ON TIME: 1 HOUR AND 20 MINUTES • TOTAL TIME: 2 HOURS • MAKES: 4–6 SERVINGS

KITCHEN GEAR
Large pot
Pot holder
Measuring cup
Sharp knife
    (adult needed)
Cutting board
Measuring spoons
Rubber spatula
    or wooden spoon
Tongs
Large bowl

INGREDIENTS
1 teaspoon olive or vegetable oil
1 onion, chopped
3 carrots, scrubbed or peeled, and diced
2 celery stalks, diced
1 garlic clove, peeled and minced or chopped
1 teaspoon dried thyme
6 cups low-sodium chicken broth
3 cups shredded or diced cooked chicken

INSTRUCTIONS
1. Put the pot on the stove and turn the heat to medium. When it is hot, carefully add the oil.
2. Add the onion, carrots, celery, garlic, and thyme and cook, stirring once or twice, until the vegetables are golden, 10 to 15 minutes.
3. Carefully pour the chicken broth into the pot. Raise the heat to high and, as soon as it boils, turn the heat to low and cook until the carrots are tender, about 30 minutes.
4. Add the chicken and stir well. Cook until the chicken is heated through, about 3 minutes.
5. Serve right away or cover and refrigerate up to 3 days.

Be Creative

Jamaican: Add 1 ¼ cups cooked or canned kidney beans and 1 ¼ cups cooked brown rice when you add the chicken.

Indian: Add 2 ½ teaspoons curry powder when you add the thyme. Add 2 tablespoons shredded coconut, 1 cup diced tomatoes (drained), 2 tablespoons fresh chopped cilantro, and 1 teaspoon fresh lemon or lime juice when you add the chicken.

French: Add 1 teaspoon dried or 1 tablespoon fresh tarragon when you add the thyme.

Greek: Add 1 teaspoon dried oregano when you add the thyme. Add 1 bunch chopped flat-leaf spinach and 2 tablespoons fresh lemon juice when you add the chicken.

A Few Great Burgers

A burger is so much more fun than a meal you eat with a knife and fork. Maybe because you get to hold it in your hands or because it reminds us of summertime barbecues, or because of all the fun toppings you can add until you get it just the way you like it. Whatever the reason, a burger's a great thing to know how to cook—and it's easy, too. If you've got an adult willing to fire up the grill, go for it—and ask them to teach you what they're doing. But a burger cooked in a skillet is supertasty, too, and it's a great way to bring a little summer feeling into the house.

We encourage you to *be creative*! A burger doesn't have to mean beef and a topping doesn't have to mean ketchup. Use your imagination to come up with your own personal best-ever burger.

Classic Beef Burger

A classic beef burger is simple and perfect and so much better than anything you can buy. Once you've mastered this recipe, running out to a fast-food restaurant will be a thing of the past. Our advice: handle the meat with a light touch because this will keep your burger tender.

ADULT NEEDED: YES · HANDS-ON TIME: 20 MINUTES · TOTAL TIME: 30 MINUTES · MAKES: 4 BURGERS

KITCHEN GEAR
Cutting board
Measuring spoons
Skillet
Sharp knife (adult needed)
Heatproof spatula

INGREDIENTS
1 pound ground beef
½ teaspoon kosher salt
¼ teaspoon black pepper
    (if you like)
4 hamburger rolls, sliced in
    half and toasted (if you like)
4 tomato slices
4 thin slices red onion
4 lettuce leaves
Ketchup, mustard, or special
    toppings (page 102)

INSTRUCTIONS
1. Put the raw meat on the cutting board and divide into 4 balls of equal size.
2. Gently press down each ball to form a patty about ¾ to 1 inch thick.
3. Using your thumb, make a ½-inch dent about the size of a quarter in the middle of each patty. (Handle the patties as little as possible, and wash your hands with soap and water after touching raw meat.)
4. Sprinkle both sides of the patties with the salt and pepper, if you like.
5. Put the skillet on the stove and turn the heat to high. Wait 2 minutes for the skillet to heat up and then carefully add the patties to the dry skillet.
6. Cook until the patties are crusty brown on the outside, about 5 minutes, then flip the patties and cook until crusty brown on the other side, another 5 minutes.
7. Put the bottom half of each roll on a big plate and top each with a burger. Top the burger with a tomato slice, onion slice, and a lettuce leaf, then cover with the top of the roll. Serve right away.

DID YOU KNOW?

Your burgers will swell in the middle as they cook, but because of the dent you've made, they'll end up about the same thickness all around. Neat, right?

Top This

- **Ketchup** (for traditionalists)
- **Mustard** (a little different)
- **Salsa** (add some spice to your life)
- **Guacamole** (page 42) (soft and creamy)
- **Classic Hummus** (page 41) (creamy and mild)
- **Cucumber Tsatsiki** (page 42) (cool and crunchy)
- **Hot Sauce** (Sriracha is a great one)
- **Pickles** (tangy)
- **Relish** (from pickley-sour to sweet)
- **Horseradish** (peppery)
- **Barbecue sauce** (from spicy to sweet)
- **Olive paste** (salty and rich)
- **Pesto** (nutty and herbal)

- **Spaghetti sauce** (page 121) (tomatoey and a little sweet)
- **Mango chutney** (sweet and tart)
- **Cranberry sauce** (sweet and tart)
- **Worcestershire sauce** (salty, sweet, and rich)

Lettuce and tomatoes are the basic burger partners, but you can also try other vegetables:

- **Raw or caramelized purple onions** (sharp-tasting raw, mellow when cooked)
- **Avocado slices** (creamy and a little sweet)
- **Marinated artichoke hearts** (tender and tangy)
- **Oven-Roasted Vegetables** (page 126) (sweet)
- **Raw or roasted red peppers** (crunchy when raw, savory when cooked)
- **Raw or roasted mushrooms** (earthy flavor)

Cheeseburgers

Classic. If you like cheese, you can't go wrong.

ADULT NEEDED: YES • HANDS-ON TIME: 25 MINUTES • TOTAL TIME: 35 MINUTES • MAKES: 4 CHEESEBURGERS

KITCHEN GEAR
Cutting board
Measuring spoons
Large skillet
Sharp knife (adult needed)

INGREDIENTS
1 pound ground beef
8 tablespoons cheese (any kind is fine)
½ teaspoon kosher salt
¼ teaspoon black pepper (if you like)
4 hamburger rolls, sliced in half and toasted (if you like)
4 tomato slices
4 thin slices red onion
4 lettuce leaves
Ketchup, mustard, or special toppings (page 102)

INSTRUCTIONS
1. Put the raw meat on the cutting board and divide into 4 balls of equal size.
2. Divide the balls in half and gently flatten each half into a disc.
3. Top half of the discs with 2 tablespoons of (or 1 small piece of) cheese. Top each cheese-topped disc with another disc. Tightly pinch the edges together and form each into a patty.
4. Gently press down to form a patty about ¾ to 1 inch thick.
5. Using your thumb, make a ½-inch dent about the size of a quarter in the middle of each side. (Handle the patties as little as possible, and wash your hands with soap and water after touching raw meat.)
6. Sprinkle both sides of the patties with the salt and pepper, if you like.
7. Put the skillet on the stove and turn the heat to high. Wait 2 minutes for the skillet to heat up and then carefully add the patties to the dry skillet.
8. Cook until the patties are crusty brown on the outside, about 5 minutes, then flip the patties and cook until crusty brown on the other side, another 5 minutes.
9. Put the bottom half of each roll on a big plate and top each with a burger. Top the burger with a tomato slice, onion slice, and a lettuce leaf. Add ketchup, mustard, or other toppings (page 102), then cover with the top of the roll. Serve right away.

Top This
- **American** (classic, buttery)
- **Cheddar** (medium sharp, medium tang—a common burger topping)
- **Monterey Jack** (mild, melts nice and smooth)
- **Mozzarella** (mild, gooey, chewy)
- **Blue** (extremely sharp, almost bites back—you need to be daring for this one)
- **Swiss** (sweet and easy)
- **Feta** (salty and tangy)
- **Goat** (creamy and tangy)

Chicken/Turkey/Pork/ Lamb Burgers

A burger will take on the personality of whatever meat you use: chicken or turkey makes a mild burger, lamb makes a very meaty-tasting one, and pork makes a burger that's almost like sausage. Experiment to find out what you like best.

ADULT NEEDED: YES • HANDS-ON TIME: 20 MINUTES • TOTAL TIME: 30 MINUTES • MAKES: 4 BURGERS

KITCHEN GEAR
Cutting board
Measuring spoons
Large skillet
Heatproof spatula

INGREDIENTS
1 pound ground chicken, turkey, pork, or lamb
½ teaspoon kosher salt
¼ teaspoon black pepper (if you like)
4 hamburger rolls, sliced in half and toasted (if you like)
4 tomato slices
4 thin slices red onion
4 lettuce leaves
Ketchup, mustard, or special toppings (page 102)

INSTRUCTIONS
1. Put the raw meat on the cutting board and divide into 4 balls of equal size.
2. Gently press down each ball to form a patty about ¾ to 1 inch thick.
3. Using your thumb, make a ½-inch dent about the size of a quarter in the middle of each side.
4. Sprinkle both sides of the patties with the salt and pepper, if you like.
5. Put the skillet on the stove and turn the heat to high. Wait 2 minutes for the skillet to heat up and then carefully add the patties to the dry skillet.
6. Cook until the patties are crusty brown on the outside, about 5 minutes, then flip the patties and cook until crusty brown on the other side, another 5 minutes.
7. Put the bottom half of each roll on a big plate and top each with a burger. Top the burger with a tomato slice, onion slice, and a lettuce leaf. Add ketchup, mustard, or other toppings (page 102), then cover with the top of the roll. Serve right away.

Salmon Burger

These are so tasty, and since the burger shape is familiar, even people who think they don't like fish might just like them!

ADULT NEEDED: YES • HANDS-ON TIME: 30 MINUTES • TOTAL TIME: 1 HOUR AND 10 MINUTES • MAKES: 4 BURGERS

KITCHEN GEAR
Cutting board
Sharp knife (adult needed)
Large mixing bowl
Large plate
Measuring spoons
Measuring cup
Large skillet
Heatproof spatula

INGREDIENTS
1–1 ½ pounds fresh salmon fillet, finely chopped
½ bunch scallions, greens and whites, chopped
1 large egg, lightly beaten
2 tablespoons olive oil
2 tablespoons Dijon mustard
3–4 tablespoons chopped fresh basil or cilantro leaves
¼ cup yellow cornmeal
1 teaspoon kosher salt
2 tablespoons whole-wheat flour
1 lemon or lime, cut into quarters
Salsa

INSTRUCTIONS
1. Put the salmon, scallions, egg, oil, mustard, and basil or cilantro in the large bowl and toss gently to combine. Don't overmix or the salmon will get mushy.
2. Put the cornmeal, salt, and flour on a large plate and mix until combined.
3. Divide the salmon mixture into 4 balls and roll them in the cornmeal mixture. Put the balls on a plate and press down to make patties. Cover and refrigerate at least half an hour and up to 8 hours.
4. Put the skillet on the stove and turn the heat to medium-high. When it is hot, carefully add the oil. Add the patties and cook until well browned, about 3 minutes on each side.
5. Serve right away with lemon or lime quarters and salsa.

Beanie Burger

This is a great meal to serve vegetarians, of course, but it's also just plain great: tasty, satisfying, and full of nutrients. Serve the burgers with any of the following: lettuce, tomato, Guacamole (page 42), salsa, Monterey Jack cheese, Cucumber Tsatsiki (page 42), plain yogurt, and lime quarters.

ADULT NEEDED: YES • HANDS-ON TIME: 30 MINUTES • TOTAL TIME: 30 MINUTES • MAKES: 4 BURGERS

KITCHEN GEAR
Can opener
Colander or strainer
Fork
Measuring cup
Sharp knife (adult needed)
Cutting board
Large mixing bowl
Large skillet
Heatproof spatula

INGREDIENTS
1 large egg
1 (16-ounce) can black beans, drained and rinsed
½ cup leftover rice, barley, or Panko bread crumbs
2 scallions, greens and whites, minced (about ¼ cup)
2 tablespoons chopped fresh cilantro or basil leaves, or a combination
1 garlic clove, peeled and minced or chopped
¼ teaspoon ground cumin, or more, to taste
¼ teaspoon dried oregano or basil
1 teaspoon olive oil
½ teaspoon kosher salt
½ teaspoon black pepper

INSTRUCTIONS
1. Crack the egg into the bowl and whisk until pale yellow. Add the beans and, using the fork, mash until chunky.
2. Add the rice, scallions, cilantro, garlic, cumin, and oregano to the egg mixture and mix until well combined.
3. Divide the mixture into 4 portions and form each into a patty about ¾ to 1 inch thick. Sprinkle the patties with salt and pepper.
4. Put the skillet on the stove and turn the heat to high. When it is hot, add the oil. Add the burgers and cook until the patties are crusty brown on both sides and heated throughout, 4 to 5 minutes per side.

Be Creative
Use chickpeas (garbanzo beans), pinto, or dark red kidney beans instead of black beans.

A Few Great Tofu Recipes

Here's the thing about tofu: although we love it, we have to admit that it can be kind of bland and spongy—but those are the very qualities that make it such a great ingredient to cook with! All it wants to do is soak up flavor, so give it delicious flavors to soak up, and you'll make a tasty and very nutritious meal. We're going to show you ways to make tofu crusty, spicy, and saucy. Once you get a sense of how it works as an ingredient, experiment to find the way you like it best! And, if you're like lots of kids, you might like to snack on raw cubes of it while you're cooking.

Sesame-Crusted Tofu

Here, tofu gets a crunchy coating from sesame seeds and a bit of savory deliciousness from soy sauce. Only four ingredients, but so, so good.

ADULT NEEDED: YES · HANDS-ON TIME: 20 MINUTES · TOTAL TIME: 30 MINUTES · MAKES: 4 SERVINGS

KITCHEN GEAR
Measuring cup
Large plate
Measuring spoons
Large skillet
Heatproof spatula

INGREDIENTS
¼ cup raw sesame seeds
1 (14–16 ounce) block firm or extra-firm tofu, drained (see below)
1 tablespoon canola or vegetable oil
1 tablespoon low-sodium soy sauce

INSTRUCTIONS
1. Put the sesame seeds on the plate. Add the drained tofu chunks, and move them around until the sides are covered with sesame seeds (don't worry if the sesame seeds don't completely coat the tofu; it doesn't matter).
2. Put the skillet on the stove and turn the heat to medium-high. When the skillet is hot, carefully add the oil. Carefully add the tofu and cook until it is golden brown, about 4 minutes per side.
3. Drizzle the soy sauce over the tofu and cook 1 more minute. Serve right away.

How to Drain Tofu
Tofu is really watery. You have to dry it out a lot before cooking it.
1. Pull the plastic off the tofu container (you may need to cut it with a knife). Carefully tip the container so that the liquid pours out of it. Put the tofu on the cutting board and cut it into 4 equal pieces, then cut each of those pieces in half the other direction to end up with 8 pieces.
2. Put a clean dish towel or 2 layers of paper towel on the cutting board and put the tofu on top. Let drain at least 20 minutes (and up to 2 hours), then put the dish towel in the wash or the paper towels in the trash.

DID YOU KNOW?

Tofu is also called "bean curd" because it's made from soybeans in a process similar to making cheese. First the beans are soaked, ground, and strained; the resulting soy milk is curdled, just like milk is curdled to make cheese. "Curdling" makes the protein coagulate, or stick together. Afterward the curds are pressed into blocks of tofu.

Curried Tofu Fingers

Try this recipe—and then try telling us that tofu isn't flavorful! Serve this dish plain or with mango chutney mixed with yogurt.

ADULT NEEDED: YES • HANDS-ON TIME: 20 MINUTES • TOTAL TIME: 1 HOUR AND 10 MINUTES • MAKES: 4 SERVINGS

KITCHEN GEAR
Measuring spoons
Baking pan
Heatproof spatula

INGREDIENTS
1 (14–16 ounce) block firm or extra-firm tofu, drained (page 108)
2 teaspoons canola or vegetable oil
2 teaspoons curry powder
½ teaspoon kosher salt

INSTRUCTIONS
1. Turn the oven on and set it to 450 degrees.
2. Put the oil, curry powder, and salt on the baking sheet and mix it around. Add the drained tofu pieces (see page 108) and gently roll them in the curry oil until all the sides are coated.
3. Put the baking sheet in the oven and bake until the tofu is just browned, about 30 minutes. Serve right away.

In Chinese mythology, the god of war, Kuan Ti, had a job **selling tofu** when he was a child. (This was before he became a god, of course.) Tofu was invented in China more than 2,000 years ago.

Ginger-Garlic Tofu

For a family-pleasing meal, serve this flavorful dish with brown rice and steamed broccoli.

ADULT NEEDED: YES • HANDS-ON TIME: 15 MINUTES • TOTAL TIME: 45 MINUTES • MAKES: 4 SERVINGS

KITCHEN GEAR
Measuring spoons
Measuring cup
Small pot
Large skillet
Heatproof spatula or tongs

INGREDIENTS
1 (14–16-ounce) block firm or extra-firm tofu, drained (see page 108)
3 tablespoons low-sodium soy sauce
⅓ cup water
1 tablespoon fresh ginger, peeled and minced
2 garlic cloves, peeled and minced or chopped
1 teaspoon toasted sesame oil (if you like)
¼ teaspoon chili pepper flakes or more, if you like it spicy
1 tablespoon canola or vegetable oil
2 tablespoons toasted sesame seeds
2 scallions, greens and whites, sliced

INSTRUCTIONS
1. Put the soy sauce, water, ginger, garlic, sesame oil (if you like), and chili pepper flakes (if you like it spicy) in the small pot.
2. Put the pot on the stove and turn the heat to high. When it comes to a boil, turn the heat down to low and cook for 10 minutes. The sauce should have halved in volume and be thicker than it was. Set aside.
3. Put the skillet on the stove and turn the heat to medium. When it is hot, carefully add the oil.
4. Add the tofu and cook until it is golden brown underneath, about 3 minutes. Using the spatula or tongs, turn the tofu over and cook until golden, 3 more minutes.
5. Add the sauce to the pan and cook 1 minute.
6. Serve right away, sprinkled with sesame seeds and scallions.

Top This
Add any of the following extras to each serving:
- 1 teaspoon chopped fresh cilantro or basil leaves
- ¼–½ teaspoon chili sauce (Sriracha)

A Few Great Make-It-Your-Way Meals

These are fun meals to serve: you give each person the bowl or plate of food, and they get to customize their own from the toppings you've put out on the table.

We've adapted four particular recipes for this style of eating: two chilies, fish tacos, fajitas, and a potato/sweet potato bar—but it's actually a good way to think about turning a simple meal into dinner. Even a very plain bowl of cooked pinto beans can be exciting, for example, if you top it with crumbled feta, diced red onion, and toasted pumpkin seeds. Plus, everyone just seems to *like* food better when they have a hand in preparing it just how they want it.

Vegetable Chili

Chili can be spicy, but this recipe is designed to be mild. If you want to go for the burn, add the extra spices listed in the ingredients section or fresh or dried chili peppers. You can use lots of different vegetables, but we especially like silky sweet butternut squash or eggplant, which adds a kind of meatiness. Be absolutely sure you cook them both until they are very soft!

ADULT NEEDED: YES • HANDS-ON TIME: 40 MINUTES • TOTAL TIME: 1 HOUR AND 40 MINUTES • MAKES: 6–8 SERVINGS

KITCHEN GEAR
Measuring spoons
Measuring cup
Cutting board
Sharp knife
   (adult needed)
Colander or strainer
Large heavy-
   bottomed pot
   with lid
Large spoon
Pot holder

Fancy That!

Add 2 cups fresh or frozen corn kernels when you add the zucchini.

INGREDIENTS
2   teaspoons olive or vegetable oil
1   large onion, chopped
3   garlic cloves, peeled and minced or chopped
3   cups peeled and diced butternut squash or eggplant
2   red, orange, or yellow bell peppers, cored, seeded, and diced
2–4 tablespoons chili powder (or more to taste)
1–1 ½ teaspoons dried oregano
1–2 teaspoons ground cumin (or more to taste)
1   teaspoon crushed red pepper flakes (if you like it spicy)
¼–½ teaspoon cayenne pepper (if you like it spicy)
¼   cup water (if you need it)
4   cups cooked or canned dark red kidney beans, drained and rinsed
2   cups cooked or canned black beans, drained and rinsed
2   (28-ounce) cans diced tomatoes, including the juice
2   small or 1 large zucchini, diced

INSTRUCTIONS
1. Put the pot on the stove and turn the heat to medium. When it is hot, carefully add the oil.
2. Add the onion, garlic, butternut squash, bell peppers, chili powder, oregano, cumin, and red pepper flakes and cayenne (if you like it spicy) and cook on low heat until the onion is soft and almost melted, about 20 minutes. Stir from time to time. If it looks dry, add the water.
3. Add the beans and tomatoes and cook, covered, stirring occasionally, for 30 minutes.
4. Add the zucchini and cook, uncovered, until the zucchini is tender, about 20 minutes.
5. Serve right away, or cover and refrigerate up to 3 days.

Top This

- Diced avocado
- Chopped fresh basil or cilantro leaves
- Grated cheddar, Monterey Jack, or goat cheese
- Yogurt, plain Greek or traditional
- Roasted or fresh bell peppers, chopped
- Chopped scallions, greens and whites
- Lemon or lime quarters, for squeezing
- Chopped onions
- Corn kernels
- Salsa or hot sauce
- Canned chipotle chiles, chopped

Try This

A lot of the fun here is in the toppings, but it can be time-consuming to do this much slicing and dicing. We recommend getting a *sous chef* (a French name for "cooking assistant") to help you do this while you focus on the recipe. Brothers, sisters, friends, uncles, neighbors, and parents are all excellent candidates for the job.

DID YOU KNOW?

Mixing beans, peppers, and spices—sometimes with meat added—was done by the Incas, Aztecs, and Mayan Indians long before European explorers like Christopher Columbus and Cortés came to the New World.

Meat Chili

This is the classic *chili con carne* (chili with meat) you've probably had before. It's a fun dish because you can make it as spicy as you like. Instead of garnishing each serving, you can put the toppings out on the table so everyone can customize their own bowls!

ADULT NEEDED: YES • HANDS-ON TIME: 45 MINUTES • TOTAL TIME: 1 ¾ HOURS • MAKES: ABOUT 12 CUPS

KITCHEN GEAR
Large heavy-bottomed pot with lid
Measuring spoons
Measuring cup
Cutting board
Sharp knife (adult needed)
Colander or strainer
Large spoon
Pot holder

INGREDIENTS
2 teaspoons olive or vegetable oil
1 large onion, chopped
2 bell peppers (any color is fine), cored, seeded, and diced
3 garlic cloves, peeled and minced or chopped
1 ¼ pounds ground turkey, chicken, beef, or pork
2–4 tablespoons chili powder
1 ½ teaspoons dried oregano
1–2 teaspoons ground cumin
1 teaspoon crushed red pepper flakes (if you like it spicy)
¼ teaspoon cayenne pepper (if you like it spicy)
4 cups cooked or canned dark red kidney beans, drained and rinsed
2 cups cooked or canned black beans, drained and rinsed
1 (28-ounce) can diced tomatoes, including the juice
1 (28-ounce) can tomato puree

INSTRUCTIONS
1. Put the pot on the stove and turn the heat to medium. When it is hot, carefully add the oil.
2. Add the onion, peppers, and garlic and cook until the onion is soft and almost melted, about 20 minutes. Stir from time to time.
3. Add the ground turkey, a little bit at a time, stirring after each addition until it just starts to change color, about 5 minutes. It is important to add the meat a little at a time, to give the liquid time to evaporate at each step. If you don't, the meat won't get hot enough to turn brown. (Remember to wash your hands with soap and water before and after handling raw meat).
4. Add the spices, stir, and cook 5 minutes.
5. Add the beans, tomatoes, and tomato puree and cook uncovered, stirring occasionally, for 30 minutes.
6. Put the lid on and cook for 30 more minutes.
7. Serve right away with the toppings (see page 115), or cover and refrigerate up to 3 days.

Potato/Sweet Potato Bar

A baked potato or sweet potato is thought of as a side dish but is really, with a little work, a great meal. Simply bake and then pile it on! *By Catherine Newman*

ADULT NEEDED: YES • HANDS-ON TIME: 20 MINUTES • TOTAL TIME: 1 HOUR AND 20 MINUTES • MAKES: 4 SERVINGS

KITCHEN GEAR
Fork
Baking sheet
Cutting board
Sharp knife (adult needed)
Pot Holder

INGREDIENTS
4 Idaho or sweet potatoes

INSTRUCTIONS
1. Turn the oven on and set it to 450 degrees.
2. Using the fork, poke a dozen or so small small holes in each potato.
3. Carefully put the potatoes directly on the rack in the hot oven. Put the baking sheet on a lower rack (this is to catch any oozy drips). Bake until tender when pushed down, about 1 hour.
4. Carefully, using a pot holder, put the potatoes on the cutting board (this is a job for an adult) and, using the fork, keep stabbing each potato to make a line down the center. Squeeze both ends to make the potato open. Serve right away with little bowls of condiments (see "Top This," left).

Top This
- Butter or olive oil and salt
- Chili (pages 112 and 114)
- Pesto
- Diced avocado
- Basil or cilantro leaves
- Grated cheddar, Monterey Jack, Parmesan, feta, or goat cheese
- Yogurt, plain Greek or traditional
- Roasted or fresh bell peppers, chopped
- Onions or scallions, greens and whites, chopped
- Lemon or lime quarters, for squeezing
- Corn kernels
- Salsa or hot sauce
- Canned chipotle chiles, chopped
- Sweet potato spices: garam masala, nutmeg, ginger, cardamom, cinnamon, curry powder

SAFETY ! TIP

The inside of the potato will be very, very hot and when you open it a lot of steam will escape, so stand back!

Fish Tacos with Purple Cabbage Slaw

There are lots of ingredients to prepare, but this isn't a hard recipe to make, and the tacos are so good. If you don't have (or like) all the taco fixings, just use what you've got! *By Catherine Newman*

ADULT NEEDED: YES • HANDS-ON TIME: 45 MINUTES • TOTAL TIME: 45 MINUTES • MAKES: 4 SERVINGS

KITCHEN GEAR
Cutting board
Sharp knife (adult needed)
Measuring cup
Measuring spoons
6 small bowls or plates
Medium-sized bowl
Large nonstick skillet
Clean dish towel
Fork
Heatproof spatula

INGREDIENTS

For assembling the tacos:
Purple Cabbage Slaw (page 118)
½ onion, finely chopped
1 medium-sized tomato, chopped
1 avocado, peeled, seeded, and diced
½ cup plain Greek yogurt
½ cup chopped fresh cilantro leaves
1 lime, quartered
Hot sauce

For the fish:
2 tablespoons olive, canola, or vegetable oil
1 teaspoon ground cumin
1 teaspoon chili powder
¼ teaspoon kosher salt
1 garlic clove, peeled and minced
1 ½ pounds firm white fish, such as halibut or cod fillets
8 (6-inch) corn tortillas

Be Creative

Chicken Tacos: instead of fish, use 1 ½ pounds chicken tenders.

INSTRUCTIONS

1. Put the Purple Cabbage Slaw (page 118), onion, tomato, avocado, yogurt, cilantro, and lime quarters in the small bowls.
2. Put the oil, spices, salt, and garlic in the medium-sized bowl and mix well.
3. Cut the fish into 1-inch strips, put them in the bowl, and use your fingers to coat them with the spice mixture. Set aside.
4. Put the skillet on the stove, turn the heat to medium, and heat the skillet for 3 minutes. Add the tortillas, one at a time, and warm them on each side for about 30 seconds. Wrap the warm tortillas in the clean dish towel to keep them warm.
5. Turn the heat up to medium-high. When the skillet is hot, add the fish and cook for 3 minutes, then use the spatula to flip the pieces over. Cook on the other side until the fish breaks easily into flakes when you poke it with a fork, about 2 minutes.
6. Give each person 2 tortillas and let everyone assemble their tacos with the ingredients they like.

Purple Cabbage Slaw

Cabbage is one of the most nutritious and delicious vegetables, so be sure to try this beautiful and hearty slaw either with fish tacos or as a great stand-alone salad. Red cabbage has a stronger taste than green, so if you aren't a cabbage eater you might want to make this with the more delicate green or Savoy cabbage first—or you could start with a bag of coleslaw mix, which is just shredded cabbage and carrots.

ADULT NEEDED: YES · HANDS-ON TIME: 20 MINUTES · TOTAL TIME: 20 MINUTES · MAKES: 8 SERVINGS

KITCHEN GEAR
Cutting board
Sharp knife (adult needed)
Box grater (adult needed)
Large bowl
Measuring cup
Measuring spoons

INGREDIENTS
1 head red cabbage
2 carrots, scrubbed or peeled, and grated
8 scallions, greens and whites, thinly sliced
¼ cup canola or vegetable oil
¼ cup unseasoned rice vinegar
½ teaspoon kosher salt
¼ teaspoon black pepper

INSTRUCTIONS
1. Cut the cabbage in half and, using the knife, finely sliver it. (This is really a job for an adult.)
2. Put all the ingredients in the bowl and toss well.
3. Cover and refrigerate at least 1 hour and up to 2 days.

Fajitas

This is a popular Mexican dish that always includes grilled meat, shrimp, or chicken and tortillas, often with grilled onions and peppers. With all the yummy add-your-own toppings, it makes a meal in itself—or serve it with a spicy black bean salad. The *j* in Spanish sounds like an *h*, so you pronounce it fah-*hee*-tahs. Be sure to marinate the meat long enough to make it tender and flavorful, but not so long that the acid in the marinade makes the meat mushy.

ADULT NEEDED: YES • HANDS-ON TIME: 35 MINUTES • TOTAL TIME: 45 MINUTES • MAKES: 6 SERVINGS

KITCHEN GEAR
Cutting board
Sharp knife (adult needed)
Measuring cup
Measuring spoons
Medium-sized shallow glass or ceramic bowl
Large skillet
Heatproof plate
Heatproof spatula or tongs
Pot holder

INGREDIENTS
1 pound boneless, skinless chicken or turkey breasts, trimmed of fat and cut into thin strips
¼ large red onion, coarsely chopped
½ cup salsa
¼ cup chopped fresh cilantro leaves
¼ cup fresh lime juice
¼ cup orange juice
¼–½ teaspoon crushed red pepper flakes
1 tablespoon vegetable or olive oil
2 red onions, thinly sliced
2 red or yellow bell peppers, cored, seeded, and thinly sliced
8–12 flour tortillas

For serving the fajitas:
Freshly chopped cilantro
Plain yogurt
1 avocado, thinly sliced
Salsa

INSTRUCTIONS
1. Put the chicken strips in the bowl and add the onion, salsa, cilantro, lime juice, orange juice, and red pepper flakes. Cover and refrigerate at least 1 hour and no more than 4 hours. Drain well, discarding all but the chicken.
2. Turn the oven on and set it to 250 degrees.
3. Put the skillet on the stove and turn the heat to medium. When it is hot, add 1½ teaspoons oil. Add the onions and peppers and cook until they begin to soften and brown, 10 to 15 minutes. Move the vegetables to the plate and put the plate in the oven to keep warm.
4. Wrap the tortillas in aluminum foil and put them in the oven to warm.
5. Using the same skillet you cooked the vegetables in, put it on the stove and turn the heat to high. Add the remaining 1 ½ teaspoons oil. Add the chicken strips and cook until they have browned, 2 to 3 minutes on each side, turning once.
6. Carefully take the plate with the peppers and tortillas out of the oven. Move the peppers to one side and add the chicken tenders.
7. Serve, buffet style, with the yogurt, avocado, and salsa on separate plates or bowls, allowing each person to assemble their own fajita.

A Few Great Pasta Dishes

Learn to cook pasta and you will always be able to feed yourself—or a crowd!
Pasta is easy to make, and the leftovers make a great school lunch. In this chapter, we're going to teach you how to make a few sauces and a few dishes. And then there's the pasta itself. In some ways, nothing could be easier: boil noodles, drain, done. But it can be a little intimidating to dump a large pot of boiling water into a colander in the sink. You will definitely need adult help in the beginning (do *not* try it alone!), and you can move on *only* when your adult feels like you've mastered being a helper. You need to be careful, and also to muster some courage! But you can do it. And it will be worth it.

Why Whole Wheat?

Whole-wheat (and other whole-grain) pasta is so much healthier for you—full of fiber and vitamins—than white pasta that we really recommend you switch to it. At first you may long for your more tender white noodles: you might want to try half white, half whole-wheat. But over time, you will learn to appreciate its flavorful, grainy goodness. And then you might want to experiment with other kinds of pasta—Asian buckwheat soba noodles, for example, which are fabulous in soup, or with a sprinkle of soy sauce, sesame seeds, and slivered scallions. Try it and see.

Basic Cooked Pasta

There are lots of ways to cook pasta but we're showing you the way we think is foolproof (a sure thing).

First, put your colander in the sink.

1. For each pound of pasta, start with a 4-quart, heavy-bottomed pot and add 1 gallon of water (when you add the pasta, be sure the water covers it by at least 2 inches).
2. If your pot has a cover, put it on (it will make the water boil faster). Bring the water to a rolling boil.
3. Carefully add the pasta and cook according to the directions on the box. Stir after it comes to a boil. Do not cover the pot.
4. Cook until *al dente*, which means "to the tooth" in Italian. That means it's thoroughly cooked, but not mushy or hard, and still offers a little bit of a bite when chewing.
5. Very carefully pour the water (you probably want to ask your adult to do this) and pasta into the colander. Continue with recipe.

World's Quickest Tomato Sauce

This easy, all-purpose tomato sauce can be used on any shape pasta, polenta, rice, quinoa, or barley. It can even be used on burgers instead of ketchup.

ADULT NEEDED: YES · HANDS-ON TIME: 20 MINUTES · TOTAL TIME: 35 MINUTES · MAKES: 4–6 SERVINGS

KITCHEN GEAR
Measuring spoons
Sharp knife (adult needed)
Measuring cup
Large skillet
Wooden spoon

INGREDIENTS
2   teaspoons olive, canola, or vegetable oil
2   garlic cloves, peeled and minced or chopped
1   tablespoon dried basil
1   teaspoon dried oregano
2 (28-ounce) cans diced tomatoes, including the liquid
2   tablespoons water
¼   cup chopped fresh basil leaves (if you like)
Shaved or grated Parmesan cheese

INSTRUCTIONS
1. Put the skillet on the stove and turn the heat to medium-low. When the skillet is hot, carefully add the oil. Add the garlic, basil, and oregano and cook for 2 minutes.
2. Add the tomatoes and water and cook until the tomato mixture starts to come together and the color is closer to orange than red, about 15 minutes.
3. Serve right away or cool, cover, and refrigerate up to 3 days.

Tip: When this sauce is completely cooled, spoon it into an ice cube tray. When the sauce has frozen, put the cubes in a freezer bag and use whenever you want.

Creamy Tomato Sauce

This takes a bit more time than many of our recipes and uses a few more ingredients, but it's well worth it. Serve with a salad and a loaf of crusty bread.

ADULT NEEDED: YES • HANDS-ON TIME: 30 MINUTES • TOTAL TIME: 1 ½ HOURS • MAKES: 4 CUPS

KITCHEN GEAR
Measuring spoons
Cutting board
Sharp knife (adult needed)
Measuring cup
Large skillet with lid
Wooden spoon

INGREDIENTS
1 tablespoon olive oil
1 red onion, diced
2 garlic cloves, peeled and minced or chopped
2 carrots, scrubbed or peeled, and diced
1 large zucchini, diced
1 red bell pepper, cored, seeded, and diced
1 tablespoon dried basil
1 (16-ounce) can diced tomatoes, including the liquid
2 tablespoons tomato paste
1 cup chicken broth or water
½ cup plain yogurt or cream (any kind is fine)
1 pound medium-shaped pasta, just cooked
½ cup chopped fresh Italian flat-leaf parsley leaves
¼ cup chopped fresh basil leaves
¼–½ cup grated Parmesan cheese

INSTRUCTIONS
1. Put the skillet on the stove and turn the heat to medium. When it is hot, add the oil. Add the onion, garlic, carrots, zucchini, pepper, and dried basil and cook until the carrots are soft and golden, 10 to 15 minutes.
2. Add the tomatoes, tomato paste, and broth or water and cook, covered, 1 hour.
3. Stir until smooth. Slowly, a little bit at a time, add the yogurt or cream, carefully stirring until heated through.
4. Add the cooked pasta, parsley, fresh basil, and Parmesan cheese and stir well. Serve right away.

Hearty Meat Sauce

This version of tomato sauces includes meat to make it a bit heartier. It can be used as an all-purpose sauce on any kind of pasta but we especially like it on Lasagna (page 124).

ADULT NEEDED: YES • HANDS-ON TIME: 30 MINUTES • TOTAL TIME: 1 ½ HOURS • MAKES: 6 CUPS

KITCHEN GEAR
Measuring spoons
Sharp knife (adult needed)
Measuring cup
Large skillet with lid
Wooden spoon

INGREDIENTS
2 teaspoons olive, canola, or vegetable oil
1 onion, chopped
2 garlic cloves, peeled and minced or chopped
1 tablespoon dried basil
1 teaspoon dried oregano
1 pound ground turkey or ground beef
2 (28-ounce) cans diced tomatoes, including the liquid
¼ cup water
¼ cup chopped fresh basil leaves (if you like)
Shaved or grated Parmesan cheese

INSTRUCTIONS
1. Put the skillet on the stove and turn the heat to medium-low. When the skillet is hot, carefully add the oil. Add the onion, garlic, basil, and oregano and cook for 2 minutes.
2. Add the ground turkey or ground beef and cook, breaking up with a spoon, until it is no longer raw, 10 to 12 minutes.
3. Add the tomatoes and water and cook the tomato mixture until it starts to come together, about 1 hour.
4. Serve right away garnished with the basil, if you like, and Parmesan, or cool, cover, and refrigerate up to 3 days.

EXPERT: Classic Lasagna

Everybody loves lasagna—maybe because it's like pizza in casserole form! It's a great meal to make for a large group, especially since all you need to do at the end is wait for it to come out of the oven. Or make it for your family, and enjoy the leftovers. Warning: No matter how many times you make this, it will never come out the same!

ADULT NEEDED: YES • HANDS-ON TIME: 30 MINUTES • TOTAL TIME: 1 ½ HOURS • MAKES 6–8 SERVINGS

KITCHEN GEAR
Measuring cup
Measuring spoons
Box grater (adult needed)
2 small mixing bowls
Wooden spoon or rubber spatula
Large baking pan
Pot holders

INGREDIENTS
2 cups ricotta cheese
½ cup low-fat or whole milk
2 large eggs
1 tablespoon dried basil, oregano, or marjoram
1 ½ cups shredded part-skim mozzarella cheese
¼ cup grated Romano cheese
¼ cup grated Parmesan cheese
½ pound no-cook lasagna noodles (these noodles have been precooked and then dried, which allows them to cook at the same rate as the rest of the lasagna)
2 ½ cups tomato sauce, Hearty Meat Sauce (page 122) or store-bought

INSTRUCTIONS
1. Turn the oven on and set it to 350 degrees.
2. Put the ricotta, milk, eggs, and basil in one of the mixing bowls. Mix well and set aside.
3. Put the mozzarella and Romano cheeses in the other mixing bowl. Mix well and set aside.
4. Put ½ cup sauce in the bottom of the pan. Cover with 3 lasagna noodles.
5. Using ⅓ of the ricotta mixture, put dollops on top of the lasagna noodles and then 1 cup tomato sauce. Repeat twice. Cover with the remaining mozzarella mixture. Add the Parmesan cheese.
6. Cover the pan with aluminum foil. Put it in the oven and cook for 40 minutes. Carefully remove the foil and cook for an additional 10 minutes. Carefully remove the pan from the oven and set aside for 10 minutes.
7. Serve right away or cool, cover with foil, and refrigerate for up to 3 days. Reheat, covered, for 45 minutes in a 350-degree oven.

Be Creative

Eggplant Lasagna: add 1 eggplant, peeled, cooked, and thinly sliced, or 3 zucchini, thinly sliced, after each tomato sauce layer.

Pesto Lasagna: add 1 cup pesto to the ricotta mixture.

Little Lasagnas

It's fun to get your own cute little lasagna! And this is an easier, quicker recipe than the big-pan lasagna. Plus, this recipe will give you some good math practice, too.

ADULT NEEDED: YES • HANDS-ON TIME: 20 MINUTES • TOTAL TIME: 1 HOUR • MAKES: 12 LITTLE LASAGNAS

KITCHEN GEAR
12-cup muffin tin
Measuring cup
Measuring spoons
Box grater (adult needed)
Pot holders
Butter knife

INGREDIENTS
½ cup hot tap water
2 ½ cups tomato sauce, World's Quickest Tomato Sauce (page 121) or store-bought
½ pound (½ box) spaghetti (any kind is fine)
¾ cup grated Parmesan cheese
1 ½ cups shredded part-skim mozzarella cheese

INSTRUCTIONS
1. Turn the oven on and set it to 350 degrees.
2. Put 2 teaspoons hot tap water in each of 12 muffin cups inside the tin.
3. Add 1 tablespoon tomato sauce to each muffin cup.
4. Count out 48 spaghetti strands. Break up 4 spaghetti strands and add them to the first muffin cup, then continue, adding 4 broken spaghetti strands to each muffin cup.
5. Top each with 1 teaspoon grated Parmesan cheese.
6. Top each with 2 teaspoons shredded mozzarella cheese.
7. Top each with 2 teaspoons tomato sauce.
8. Repeat, starting with step 4 (the spaghetti strands).
9. Repeat again.
10. Carefully put the muffin tin in the oven and bake until the top is golden and the tomato sauce is bubbling, about 45 minutes. Set aside for 10 minutes. Slide the butter knife into the inner edge of each muffin cup and gently go around it, loosening up the sides. Carefully remove the lasagnas from the tin and serve right away.

DID YOU KNOW?

Even though lasagna is an Italian pasta dish, one theory is that the word *lasagna* comes from the *Greek* word *lasanon*, which means "cooking pot." The word "lasagna" now refers to what was commonly cooked in the pot, rather than the pot itself.

A Few Great Vegetable Recipes

Raw veggies are great, but not all veggies are great raw. There are many ways to cook vegetables and while almost all are delicious, we want to teach you the methods we think are the simplest, most versatile, and bring out the best flavor and texture. As diehard veggie lovers, we can't help thinking that when kids (or grown-ups) say they don't like this or that veggie, they just haven't had it prepared well! Which doesn't mean you can't hang on to a particular dislike (maybe eggplant is just never going to be your thing), but it does mean that you can open your mind and make dishes so great that you can encourage everyone else to do the same.

Our goal here is not to teach you every vegetable dish we know. (We know so, so many!) We just want to lead you onto the path so that you can go in any direction you want to go.

Oven-Roasted Vegetables

Oven roasting is a great way to cook vegetables and can easily turn a vegetable hater into a vegetable lover. So often vegetables are overcooked and lose their unique texture and flavor. But when you roast vegetables in the oven, you cook them for a short time at a very high heat, which brings out their richness and depth. The inside kind of melts, the flavor sweetens and concentrates, and the outside gets crisp and caramelized (that's the plant's natural sugar caramelizing—proof, if you needed it, that veggies really are sweet!). For all of you who say you don't like vegetables, we dare you to roast them.

ADULT NEEDED: YES • HANDS-ON TIME: 20 MINUTES • TOTAL TIME: UP TO 1 HOUR • MAKES: 4 SERVINGS

KITCHEN GEAR
Cutting board
Sharp knife (adult needed)
Large mixing bowl
Large rimmed baking sheet
Measuring spoons
Large spoon or spatula
Pot holder

INGREDIENTS
1½ pounds vegetable(s) of your choice (see page 128)
1 tablespoon olive oil, plus 1 teaspoon for oiling the baking sheet
½ teaspoon kosher salt
¼ teaspoon black pepper

INSTRUCTIONS
1. Turn the oven on and set it to 425 degrees. With a paper towel or your hand, lightly coat the baking sheet with oil.
2. Put the vegetable, oil, salt, and pepper in the bowl and mix well.
3. Dump the contents of the bowl onto the baking sheet, making sure the vegetables are in a single layer.
4. Carefully put the baking sheet in the oven and bake until the vegetables are deeply colored on the outside and tender on the inside, about 20 minutes to 1 hour, depending on the vegetable.
5. Serve right away, or cover and refrigerate up to 2 days.

Important Rules for Roasting:

- Arrange the vegetables in a single layer so that all the edges are exposed to the heat.
- Don't crowd them, or they'll steam instead of roast.
- Cut the vegetables all the same size, so that they'll cook evenly. The smaller they are the more caramelized they will get.
- If the vegetables start to brown too much, lower the heat to 350 degrees.
- If the vegetables aren't brown by the time they're tender, raise the heat to 500 degrees.
- Use your imagination. You can eat roasted vegetables hot or cold, alone or paired with pasta or rice, and even in frittatas and sandwiches.

The Vegetables:

How to cut and what to add before and after cooking:

Acorn Squash
Halve and scrape out the seeds. Cut into wedges, or cook the halves cut-side down.

Time in oven: 45 minutes–1 hour

Good additions before roasting include fresh thyme leaves, honey, or real maple syrup.

Asparagus
Leave whole but snap off the woody end.

Time in oven: 15–20 minutes

Good additions after roasting include a squeeze of lemon and/or a sprinkle of chopped tarragon leaves.

Beets
Use small beets or quarter large ones and wrap in aluminum foil.

Time in oven: 45 minutes–1 hour

Good additions after roasting include a splash of vinegar, a dollop of plain yogurt, or feta, goat, or blue cheese.

Broccoli, Cauliflower
Use 1 head broccoli or cauliflower. Snap off the florets and if necessary, break into 2-inch pieces. Chop the stalk into similarly sized pieces.

Time in oven: 35–45 minutes

Good additions after roasting include a squeeze of lemon, grated Parmesan cheese, or a drizzle of sesame oil.

Brussels Sprouts
Trim the ends. Leave whole if small, halve if large, and roast cut-side down.

Time in oven: 20–25 minutes

Good additions before roasting include a drizzle of real maple syrup, or after, a squeeze of lemon juice.

Cabbage
Cut half a green cabbage into ¾-inch slices, then cut into 2-inch pieces. Try to keep the cabbage together as you season it and lay it on the pan.

Time in oven: 45 minutes–1 hour, flipping the pieces with a spatula halfway through

Good additions after roasting includes a splash of balsamic vinegar or a squeeze of lemon juice.

The bottom ends of asparagus stalks are stringy and tough. To remove them, bend each raw stalk until it snaps. It'll break off in just the right spot.

Carrots, Parsnips

Trim the ends and peel if they can't be scrubbed clean. Quarter lengthwise.

Time in oven: 40 minutes

Good additions before roasting include a sprinkle of fresh thyme, rosemary, or chopped garlic; or a splash of balsamic vinegar, added after.

Mushrooms

Trim the stems. Leave whole or cut in half and roast cut-side down.

Time in oven: 20–30 minutes

Good additions before roasting include a sprinkle of dried thyme or rosemary, or chopped garlic; or a sprinkle of fresh basil, added after.

Sweet Potatoes, Potatoes

Cut into 1-inch chunks, wedges, or "fries." Don't peel unless the skins can't be scrubbed clean.

Time in oven: 45 minutes–1 hour

Good additions before roasting include a sprinkle of fresh rosemary, thyme, and/or chopped garlic.

Tomatoes, Plum or Cherry

Leave cherry tomatoes whole. Cut plum tomatoes in half and roast cut-side down.

Time in oven: 20–25 minutes

Good additions before roasting include chopped garlic or a sprinkle of dried thyme; or chopped fresh basil and/or crumbled feta, added after.

Zucchini, Summer Squash

Trim the ends. Cut into slices or "fries."

Time in oven: 20–30 minutes

Good additions after roasting include a sprinkle of chopped basil, mint, or parsley, or a squeeze of lemon.

On average a person eats 10,866 carrots during their lifetime. Carrots can be purple, white, yellow, red, and black as well as orange; their color is affected by temperature, the season when they're grown, soil content, water, and the amount of daylight.

Pan Roasting

Pan roasting is similar to oven roasting: you use high heat and cook for a short amount of time. It's an especially good way to cook more-delicate vegetables, since they don't brown as much as they do in the oven. It's also a great way to make the most of a little bit of oil: instead of frying the vegetables, which would use *a lot* of oil, you concentrate their flavor quickly in a spoonful of hot oil, before letting them finish cooking more gently with a splash of water. Unlike steaming, which can water down a vegetable's flavor, this method intensifies all the flavor and sweetness that's already there. Try it with one of the three veggies we show here—or experiment with one we don't!

Pan-Roasted Asparagus

The asparagus comes out sweet, tender, and perfect.

ADULT NEEDED: YES • HANDS-ON TIME: 15 MINUTES • TOTAL TIME: 15 MINUTES • MAKES: 2–4 SERVINGS

KITCHEN GEAR
Large skillet
Measuring spoons

INGREDIENTS
1 bunch asparagus, woody end snapped off
2 tablespoons cold tap water
1 teaspoon olive oil
¼ lemon

INSTRUCTIONS
1. Put the asparagus, water, and oil in the skillet and turn the heat to high.
2. Bring to a boil and cook until the water has been absorbed and the asparagus starts to sizzle, about 5 minutes. (Sizzling food makes a hissing or frying sound.)
3. Remove the asparagus from the skillet. Squeeze the lemon over the asparagus and serve right away.

Asparagus Debate
Some people think the tastiest asparagus are the fattest ones. Others prefer the slim kind. What do you think?

One kind of asparagus is white. It becomes pale because it is covered up and grown without sunlight.

Pan-Roasted Green Beans

This recipe is so delicious you won't be able to stop eating it—and you don't need to! It makes a great side dish for just about anything, and the beans are good at room temperature or cold, too.

ADULT NEEDED: YES • HANDS-ON TIME: 20 MINUTES • TOTAL TIME: 20 MINUTES • MAKES: 4 SERVINGS

KITCHEN GEAR
Sharp knife (adult needed)
Cutting board
Measuring spoons
Measuring cup
Large skillet
Heatproof spatula or wooden spoon

INGREDIENTS
1 teaspoon olive oil
2 garlic cloves, peeled and minced
1 tablespoon finely chopped fresh ginger (if you like)
1 pound green beans, washed and trimmed
¼ teaspoon kosher salt
¼ cup cold water

INSTRUCTIONS
1. Put the skillet on the stove and turn the heat to low.
2. Add the oil. When the oil is hot, add the garlic and ginger, if you like, and cook until they are just turning golden, about 30 seconds.
3. Add the beans and salt and stir until they are lightly coated with the oil.
4. Add the water, raise the heat to high, and cook until the skillet is almost dry, about 6 minutes. Serve right away.

Fancy That!
- Stir in 1 teaspoon Dijon mustard
- Add 1 tablespoon chopped toasted almonds or walnuts
- Add 1 tablespoon chopped fresh basil or cilantro leaves
- Add ½ teaspoon crushed red pepper flakes (if you like it spicy)

DID YOU KNOW?

Green beans are packed with vitamins! One cup of green beans (that's equal to one serving) provides vitamins A, C, K, and B!

Pan-Roasted Brussels Sprouts

Here's a recipe that's sure to take any Brussels-sprouts haters from "yuck" to "yum"! Although, to be honest, we've found that more and more people are turning out to like this vegetable, which looks like a dollhouse-sized head of cabbage.

ADULT NEEDED: YES • HANDS-ON TIME: 15 MINUTES • TOTAL TIME: 15 MINUTES • MAKES: 4 SERVINGS

KITCHEN GEAR
Cutting board
Sharp knife (adult needed)
Measuring cup
Wooden spoon
Measuring spoon
Skillet with lid

INGREDIENTS
1 pound Brussels sprouts, trimmed and quartered

½ cup water

2 teaspoons olive oil

1 teaspoon low-sodium soy sauce or balsamic vinegar

INSTRUCTIONS
1. Put the Brussels sprouts, water, and oil in the skillet and turn the heat to high.
2. Bring to a boil, cover and cook 2 minutes.
3. Remove the lid carefully and add the soy sauce or vinegar. Cook until the Brussels sprouts are just tender and lightly browned, about 5 minutes. Serve right away.

Fancy That!
Add a little bit of lemon zest, orange zest, or grated Parmesan cheese.

And a few others...

Oven roasting and pan roasting are our most versatile vegetable-cooking methods, but there are a few other recipes we just have to share! Artichokes—well, we have to include an artichoke, because there's just nothing like them! And we can't resist a couple of our favorite potato recipes, which are great for holiday dinners or weekend suppers.

Artichokes

Artichokes are in the prickly family of plants called thistles, which might explain why they look so crazy—covered in spiky leaves, like a cross between a vegetable and a dinosaur. Here's how to cook and eat one.

ADULT NEEDED: YES • HANDS-ON TIME: 20 MINUTES • TOTAL TIME: 1 HOUR • MAKES: 1 ARTICHOKE PER PERSON

KITCHEN GEAR
Large pot with lid

Sharp knife (adult needed)

Cutting board

Clean scissors

Colander

INGREDIENTS
1 artichoke per person

1 tablespoon unsalted butter, melted, with a squeeze of lemon, or your favorite salad dressing, for dipping

INSTRUCTIONS
1. Fill the pot halfway with water and put it on the stove. Put the lid on and turn the heat to high.

2. Use the knife to saw off an inch or so at the tip of each artichoke and all but an inch or so of its stem (this is a job for an adult). Use the clean scissors to snip any remaining pointy tips off each outer leaf, so you won't poke yourself when you eat them.

3. When the water is boiling, carefully put the artichokes in, cover the pot, and turn the heat down to low. Cook the artichokes 30 to 45 minutes depending on how big the artichoke is. The leaves should pull out easily when you tug them.

4. Drain and cool the artichokes upside down in a colander for 10 minutes. Serve with the melted butter or salad dressing.

How to eat an artichoke

Starting with the outside leaves, pull off one leaf at a time, then dip the pale bottom of the leaf in melted butter or salad dressing, and scrape the meaty part off the inside of the leaf with your bottom teeth. You'll throw away the rest of the leaf, but you can put it in a bowl for now. Do this with all the leaves until you get to the hairy part of the artichoke (known as the "choke"), and then use a spoon to scoop out and throw away the fuzzy choke. Cut up the heart and eat it. It's the best part!

Twice-Baked Potatoes

The ricotta and cheddar cheese don't just add yummy flavor here—they also add lots of protein, which means you can serve these potatoes with a green salad and call it dinner.

ADULT NEEDED: YES • HANDS-ON TIME: 20 MINUTES • TOTAL TIME: 2 HOURS • MAKES: 4 SERVINGS

KITCHEN GEAR
Fork
Pot holders
Sharp knife (adult needed)
Spoon
Mixing bowl
Measuring cup
Small baking pan

INGREDIENTS
2 Idaho (or other thick-skinned) potatoes, scrubbed clean
¼ cup ricotta or goat cheese
¼ cup low-fat or whole milk
¼ cup shredded cheddar cheese
A pinch kosher salt

INSTRUCTIONS
1. Turn the oven on and set it to 450 degrees.
2. Using the fork, poke a dozen or so small holes in each potato.
3. When the oven is hot, put the potatoes directly on the middle rack of the oven. Bake until the potatoes are tender, about 40 minutes.
4. Using pot holders, take the potatoes out of the oven and when they are cool enough to handle, cut each potato in half with a knife.
5. With the spoon, carefully scoop out the white, inner part of the potatoes, but try not to break the skin. Put the white part in the bowl. Set the potato skins aside.
6. Add the ricotta, milk, cheddar cheese, and salt and mash together.
7. Divide the mixture into 4 piles, and scoop each pile into 1 of the potato skins.
8. Put the stuffed potatoes in the baking pan. Put the baking pan in the oven and bake until the potatoes are warmed throughout and the tops are golden, about 20 minutes.

DID YOU KNOW?

The moisture inside a potato expands when you cook it. By pricking the raw potato's skin, you give the moisture a way to escape. If you forget to do this, the potato can explode all over your oven!

Mashed Potatoes or Sweet Potatoes

We love the plainest plain mashed potatoes—and the fanciest fancy ones! That's why we're giving you so many variations and options to try. Choose sweet potatoes or regular potatoes (russet, Yukon gold, or red potatoes all work great), depending on what you like or what you think will go best with your meal.

ADULT NEEDED: YES • HANDS-ON TIME: 15 MINUTES • TOTAL TIME: 35 MINUTES • MAKES 4–6 SERVINGS

KITCHEN GEAR
Cutting board
Sharp knife (adult needed)
Large pot
Measuring cup
Measuring spoons
Colander
Potato masher or fork

INGREDIENTS
2 pounds potatoes or sweet potatoes, scrubbed or peeled and cut into large (around 2-inch) chunks
Cold water, to cover
½ cup low-fat or whole milk, Greek yogurt, or sour cream
2 tablespoons olive oil or butter
½ teaspoon kosher salt
¼ teaspoon black pepper

INSTRUCTIONS
1. Put the potatoes in the pot and put the pot on the stove. Cover the potatoes by at least 1 inch with water.
2. Turn the heat to high and bring the water to a boil. Lower the heat to medium and cook the potatoes until they're tender, about 15 minutes.
3. Dump the potatoes into the colander (this is a job for an adult).
4. Put the potatoes in the bowl and add the milk, yogurt, or sour cream, olive oil or butter, salt and pepper.
5. Using a masher or a fork, mash until smooth or chunky-smooth, depending on how you like them. Serve right away.

Or Else
Cheesy Potatoes: add ½ cup grated Parmesan or cheddar cheese when you mash them.
Leeky Potatoes: add 2 leeks (just the white part, chopped) to the potatoes before you cook them.
Sweet Potato-Carrot: substitute 1 pound carrots for 1 pound sweet potatoes.
Sweet Sweet Potato: add 2 tablespoons real maple syrup or honey when you mash, and skip the yogurt.
Green Potatoes: add 1 bunch kale, chopped, to the potatoes after they've been cooking for 10 minutes.
Turnip Potatoes: substitute 1 pound turnips for 1 pound potatoes.
Nutty Sweet Potatoes: sprinkle each serving of mashed sweet potatoes with 1 tablespoon chopped toasted pecans or walnuts.
Mashed Cauliflower: substitute 1 large head cauliflower for the potatoes.

Dessert

Almost everybody loves dessert, so it can be lots of fun to make the sweet ending to your meal.

Of course, we think a piece of fruit is itself a lovely and satisfying dessert—but we understand that you might feel otherwise, so we're offering you our best recipes for simple showstoppers. And yes, lots of them use fruit—but just wait until you taste the kinds of extravagant treats you can make with them. You'll never look at an apple the same way again.

Melting Apples

When you bake apples, the skin keeps its shape (more or less), but the inside gets nice and tender, so you can spoon out delicious bites of melted apple. In this recipe, we've scented the apples with cinnamon and stuffed them with a mixture of dried fruit and nuts.

ADULT NEEDED: YES · HANDS-ON TIME: 20 MINUTES · TOTAL TIME: 1 HOUR AND 20 MINUTES · MAKES: 6 SERVINGS

KITCHEN GEAR
Cutting board
Melon baller or spoon
Fork
Small bowl
Sharp knife (adult needed)
Muffin tin or small baking dish
Measuring spoons
Measuring cup
Pot holder

INGREDIENTS
6   Granny Smith or other tart apples, top ⅓ of the apple cut off (feel free to eat it)
¼   cup dried fruit, like raisins, dried cranberries, currants, or chopped apricots
¼   cup coarsely chopped nuts, like toasted walnuts, pecans, or almonds
1   tablespoon real maple syrup
½   teaspoon ground cinnamon
¼   cup water

INSTRUCTIONS
1. Turn the oven on and set it to 375 degrees.
2. Put the apples on the cutting board and remove the core by using a melon baller or a spoon.
3. Lightly prick the top of the sides of the apple with a fork (this prevents the apples from splitting).
4. Put the dried fruit, nuts, real maple syrup, and cinnamon in a small bowl. Divide the mixture into 4 parts and stuff it inside the apples.
5. Put the water in the muffin tin or baking dish. Add the apples. Carefully put the baking dish in the oven and bake until the apples are soft, about 1 hour.
6. Serve right away or cover and refrigerate up to 2 days.

Be Creative

Baked Pears: Substitute pears for the apples.

Desserts are different in different parts of the world: In China, a thin, sweet red bean soup is a common dessert. It is served hot in the winter and cold in the summer. In France, a small cake called a *canelé*—with a sweet, crisp, brown outside and a moist, creamy, puddinglike inside—is a common baked treat. In the Middle East, baklava is served. Baklava is constructed from many paper-thin layers of crunchy dough, called "filo," layered with nuts (often pistachios) and drizzled with syrup or honey.

Best-Ever (You'll Never Buy Jars Again) Applesauce

This recipe will give you such a good I-can't-believe-I-made-it-from-scratch feeling! Maybe because maple and apple trees grow in the same climate, the two flavors taste delicious together. Eat this plain, spoon it into yogurt, or eat it alongside chicken, pork, or potato pancakes.

ADULT NEEDED: YES • HANDS-ON TIME: 15 MINUTES • TOTAL TIME: 45 MINUTES • MAKES: 4 SERVINGS

KITCHEN GEAR
Sharp knife (adult needed)
Cutting board
Measuring cup
Measuring spoons
Medium-sized pot with lid
Wooden spoon
Potato masher or fork
Container with lid

INGREDIENTS
4 Granny Smith or other tart apples, cored, peeled (if you like), and diced
¼ cup water
3 tablespoons real maple syrup

INSTRUCTIONS
1. Put the apples, water, and real maple syrup in the pot, cover, and put on the stove. Turn the heat to medium-low and cook until the apples are tender, about 30 minutes, stirring occasionally to make sure the apples aren't sticking. Set aside to cool a bit, about 10 minutes.
2. Mash the apples using a potato masher or fork until chunky (if you like it smoother, mash some more) and set aside to cool until just warm.
3. Serve right away, or put it in the container and refrigerate until cold.

Be Creative
- **Chunky Nutty Applesauce:** Add ½ cup chopped toasted walnuts or pecans.
- **Chunky Nutty Fruity Applesauce:** Add ½ cup chopped toasted walnuts or pecans and ¼ cup raisins, currants, or diced apricots or prunes.
- **Cranberry Applesauce:** Add ½ cup fresh or frozen cranberries when you add the apples.
- **Rhubarb Applesauce:** Add ½ cup chopped cooked rhubarb when you add the apples.
- **Banana Applesauce:** Add 1 overripe banana after you cook the apples, and mash them together.
- **Pearsauce:** Substitute pears for the apples.

Fruit Crisp

A crisp is kind of like a pie—only instead of a crust on the bottom, it has a crispy and delicious granolalike mixture on the top. Once you learn how to make it, it becomes fun to adapt the recipe to use whatever fruits are in season.

ADULT NEEDED: YES • HANDS-ON TIME: 20 MINUTES • TOTAL TIME: 1 HOUR AND 20 MINUTES • MAKES: 8 SERVINGS

KITCHEN GEAR
Cutting board
Sharp knife (adult needed)
Measuring cup
Measuring spoons
Mixing bowl
Pie plate
Mixing spoon
Heatproof spatula
Pot holder

INGREDIENTS
For the fruit filling:
5–6 apples, scrubbed (and peeled, if you like), cored, and chopped
2 tablespoons sweetener, like real maple syrup, honey, or sugar
1 tablespoon flour (any kind is fine)
½ teaspoon ground cinnamon

For the crisp topping:
¾ cup flour (any kind is fine)
¾ cup old-fashioned oats
⅓ cup unsalted butter, melted
3 tablespoons sugar
¼ teaspoon kosher salt

INSTRUCTIONS
1. Turn the oven on and set it to 350 degrees.
2. To make the fruit filling: Put the apples, sweetener, flour, and cinnamon in the pie plate and stir well.
3. To make the crisp topping: Put the flour, oats, butter, sugar, and salt in the mixing bowl and mix until it looks like little pebbles.
4. Pour the crisp topping on the filling and using your clean hands, move it around until the apples are evenly covered.
5. Carefully put the pie plate in the oven and bake until the topping is lightly browned and the apples are tender, about 1 hour.
6. Set aside to cool a little bit. Serve warm or at room temperature or refrigerate and serve cold.

Why do you add flour to the filling of a crisp or pie? A lot of juice seeps out of the fruit as it cooks. The flour combines with the juice to thicken it, forming a kind of sauce so that the dessert doesn't end up mushy or liquidy. Some people (your grandma, for one) might use tapioca or cornstarch to do the same thing.

Be Creative
- **Strawberry-Rhubarb:** Substitute 1 pound rhubarb, halved lengthwise and thinly sliced, and 1 quart strawberries, cut into quarters, for the apples. Leave out the ground cinnamon.
- **Pear-Ginger:** Substitute 6 ripe pears, cored, cut into quarters and thinly sliced, for the apples. Add 2 teaspoons finely chopped fresh ginger. Substitute nutmeg for the cinnamon.
- **Peach:** Substitute 6 ripe peaches, cut into quarters and thinly sliced, for the apples.
- **Nectarine, Strawberry, and Blueberry:** Instead of apples, use 4 nectarines, pitted, peeled, and cut, 1 pint strawberries, cut into quarters, and 1 pint blueberries. Leave out the ground cinnamon.

Banana-Peach Frozen Yogurt

The most popular fruit in the United States, bananas can be found in most households. We recommend you keep a few sliced bananas (as well as berries) in your freezer so you can make this simple and speedy dessert anytime. If you don't have a food processor but do have a blender, it's okay to use it. It's just a little harder to get all the yogurt out.

ADULT NEEDED: YES · HANDS-ON TIME: 10 MINUTES · TOTAL TIME: 10 MINUTES · MAKES 4 SERVINGS

KITCHEN GEAR
Cutting board
Sharp knife (adult needed)
Measuring spoons
Measuring cup
Food processor (adult needed)

INGREDIENTS
2 overripe bananas (see page 5), thinly sliced and frozen
2 cups chopped frozen peaches
½ teaspoon vanilla extract
⅓ cup plain yogurt

INSTRUCTIONS
1. Put the frozen bananas and peaches in the bowl of the food processor fitted with a steel blade and put the top on tightly.
2. Turn the machine on and process until smooth. Gradually add the vanilla extract and yogurt and process until completely incorporated. Serve right away.

Be Creative
- **Mango:** Substitute mangoes or papaya for the peaches.
- **Tropical:** Substitute fresh or frozen pineapple chunks for the peaches and 1 teaspoon grated fresh lime zest for the vanilla extract.
- **Berry:** Substitute 4 cups frozen berries, including raspberries, strawberries, blueberries, and/or blackberries, for the peaches and bananas. Substitute 1 teaspoon lemon juice for the vanilla extract.

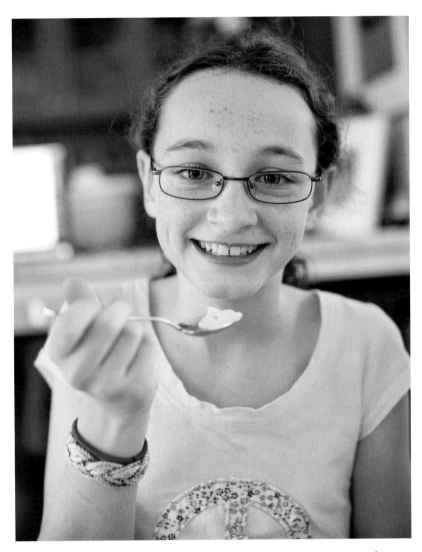

Why do bananas turn brown? There's an enzyme in banana peels called tyrosinase, and when it gets exposed to air over time, it reacts with the oxygen and turns brown—just like a cut apple, and a little bit like rusting metal.

DID YOU KNOW?

Banana "trees" are actually herbs. The bananas grow upward, against gravity.

EXPERT: Impressive Fruit Tart

This kind of tart, with a free-form crust that's not pressed into a pie plate, is called a *galette*, which is French for, um, this kind of tart. You can use any fruit that is in season—and if you feel adventurous, you can even make a dinner galette substituting cooked vegetables, grated cheese, and herbs for the filling.

ADULT NEEDED: YES • HANDS-ON TIME: 25 MINUTES • TOTAL TIME: 1 ½ HOURS • MAKES: 4–6 SERVINGS

KITCHEN GEAR
Mixing bowl
Measuring cup
Measuring spoons
Baking sheet
Rolling pin
Sharp knife (adult needed)
Pot holders

INGREDIENTS
For the dough:

½ cup all-purpose flour

½ cup whole-wheat flour

¼ teaspoon kosher salt

6 tablespoons unsalted butter, chilled or frozen and cut into 12 pieces

4 tablespoons ice water

For the filling:

2 tablespoons all-purpose flour

¼ cup sugar

6–8 plums or apricots or 4–6 pears or peaches, pitted and very thinly sliced

INSTRUCTIONS
1. To make the dough: Put the flour, salt, and butter in the bowl and massage them together with your clean fingers until the mixture looks like little pills. Be patient and gentle; this will take a little while to get the hang of.
2. Add the water, 1 tablespoon at a time, massage some more, and form the dough into a ball. Flatten into a large disc, cover with plastic wrap, and refrigerate 1 hour.
3. Turn the oven on and set it to 400 degrees.
4. To assemble the tart: Take the disc out of the refrigerator and put it on a baking sheet.
5. Using a rolling pin, roll the dough into a 15-inch circle (it doesn't have to be exact). Sprinkle the flour in the center, leaving a 2-inch border all around (this means: don't sprinkle the flour on the outermost 2 inches).
6. Lay the fruit slices over the flour, overlapping them as needed to fit them all. Sprinkle the top with 2 tablespoons sugar.
7. Fold up the dough border to partially cover the fruit and pinch and seal the edges where possible.
8. Brush the visible dough with water and sprinkle the remaining 2 tablespoons sugar on the top of the dough.
9. Carefully put the baking sheet in the oven and bake until the top is lightly browned and the fruit is bubbling, 35 to 50 minutes. Set aside to cool and serve warm or at room temperature.

Brownies

These brownies are not run of the mill: they're made with whole-wheat flour, which makes them nutty, rich, and amazingly yummy.

ADULT NEEDED: YES • HANDS-ON TIME: 20 MINUTES • TOTAL TIME: 1 HOUR • MAKES: 16 SQUARES

KITCHEN GEAR
9 x 12-inch baking pan
Measuring cup
Small pot
Rubber spatula or heatproof spoon
Measuring spoons
Large mixing bowl
Pot holder

INGREDIENTS
Canoa or vegetable oil (for oiling the pan)
4 ounces unsweetened chocolate
2 sticks unsalted butter
1 ½ cups sugar
4 large eggs, at room temperature
1 tablespoon vanilla extract
1 cup whole-wheat flour
½ teaspoon kosher salt
1–2 cups toasted walnuts or pecans, coarsely chopped (if you like)

INSTRUCTIONS
1. Turn the oven on and set it to 325 degrees. Using your clean hand or a paper towel, lightly coat the pan with canola or vegetable oil.
2. Put the chocolate and butter in the pot and put it on the stove. Turn the heat to very low and cook until both have melted, about 5 minutes. Stir with the spatula and set aside to cool to room temperature.
3. Put the sugar, eggs, and vanilla extract in the bowl and beat until it looks creamy yellow and frothy, 1 to 2 minutes.
4. Add the cooled chocolate mixture and mix until just combined.
5. Add the flour and salt and mix again until well combined. Add the nuts, if you like, and gently combine.
6. Scrape the mixture out of the bowl and into the prepared pan.
7. Carefully put the pan in the oven and bake 25 minutes. Set aside to cool completely. Cut into 16 squares.

DID YOU KNOW?

Unlike many other recipes, brownies are a relatively recent invention. Some say they were so named because they contained molasses, not chocolate, which turned them dark brown. Later, chocolate was added. They became popular at the end of the nineteenth century, as chocolate became widely available in America.

Banana Bread

Banana bread is classic and delicious, and another great way to use up bananas that are a little past their prime for eating. If you like, divide the mixture into a 12-cup muffin tin and when they're done, call them cupcakes or muffins! (Just note: In a muffin tin, they won't need to cook as long—be sure to check them at 20 minutes.)

ADULT NEEDED: YES • HANDS-ON TIME: 20 MINUTES • TOTAL TIME: 1 HOUR • MAKES: 12 SLICES

KITCHEN GEAR
Measuring cup
Measuring spoons
Mixing bowl
Large spoon or rubber spatula
Loaf pan
Pot holder

INGREDIENTS
1   cup all-purpose flour
½ cup whole-wheat flour
1 ½ teaspoons baking soda
½ teaspoon kosher salt
3–4 overripe bananas
1   cup sugar
1   stick unsalted butter, melted and cooled, or ½ cup canola or vegetable oil (plus extra for oiling the pan)
2   large eggs, at room temperature
2   teaspoons vanilla extract
½ cup chopped toasted walnuts or pecans (if you like)

INSTRUCTIONS
1. Turn the oven on and set it to 350 degrees. Using your clean hand or a paper towel, lightly oil the pan with canola or vegetable oil.

2. Put the flour, baking soda, and salt in the bowl and mix well. Set aside.

3. Put the bananas and sugar in the bowl and mash, mash, mash, until the mixture is completely smooth and there are no big chunks of banana.

4. Add the butter or oil, eggs, and vanilla extract and mix well.

5. Add the flour mixture, a little at a time, and mix well.

6. Add the nuts, if you like, and mix again.

7. Pour the mixture into the prepared pan and carefully put it in the oven. Bake until firm in the center, 1 hour. Set aside to cool, and serve warm or at room temperature.

Why do you use overripe bananas in banana bread? We know, they're kind of gross looking! But the banana plant stores its energy as starches, which are converted to sugars as the fruit ripens. So the riper the banana, the sweeter it tastes—even if it becomes so ripe that it turns polka-dotted!

Be Creative

**Black Cocoa
Banana Bread:**
Instead of 1 cup
all-purpose flour,
use ½ cup flour and
1 cup unsweetened
cocoa powder.

Yellow Cupcakes with Chocolate Ganache

Who doesn't like cupcakes? These easy-to-make, totally yummy cupcakes can be topped with a little bit of confectioners' sugar (for those who don't like icing), homemade whipped cream (for those who like things simple), or with some ganache (for those who love the intensity of rich chocolate). Feel free to decorate however you like!

ADULT NEEDED: YES • HANDS-ON TIME: 20 MINUTES • TOTAL TIME: 45 MINUTES • MAKES: 12 CUPCAKES

KITCHEN GEAR
12-cup muffin tin
Paper or foil liners
Measuring cup
Measuring spoons
Small bowl
Large bowl
Mixing spoons
Pot holder
Rubber spatula

INGREDIENTS
1 ½ cups all-purpose flour
1 ½ teaspoons baking powder
½ teaspoon kosher salt
1 stick unsalted butter, at room temperature
1 cup sugar
1 large egg, at room temperature
2 large egg yolks, at room temperature
1 ½ teaspoons vanilla extract
½ cup plain whole-milk yogurt or sour cream

INSTRUCTIONS
1. Turn the oven on and set it to 350 degrees. Line the muffin tin with paper or foil liners.
2. Put the flour, baking powder, and salt in the small bowl and mix well.
3. Put the butter, sugar, egg, egg yolks, vanilla extract, and yogurt or sour cream in the large bowl and mix until smooth and satiny, about 30 seconds. Scrape down the sides of the bowl with the spatula and mix again.
4. Add the flour mixture and mix until well combined.
5. Using a heaping tablespoon, divide the batter evenly among the cupcake liners.
6. Carefully put the tin in the oven and bake until the tops are just beginning to color but not brown, 20 to 24 minutes. Set aside to cool.

What is ganache? It comes from the French word for "glaze," and it's just a fancy name for frosting, except that instead of using lots of butter and sugar, it's made from chocolate and cream. In addition to topping cupcakes, an even more chocolatey version of ganache is often used as a filling in truffles and pastries.

Chocolate Ganache

Feel free to substitute the semisweet chocolate with bittersweet, milk, or white chocolate—each tastes great!

ADULT NEEDED: YES • HANDS-ON TIME: 20 MINUTES • TOTAL TIME: 1 HOUR AND 5 MINUTES • MAKES: 12 CUPCAKES

KITCHEN GEAR
Measuring cup
Small pot
Medium-sized bowl
Large spoon or whisk
Plate

INGREDIENTS
½ cup heavy cream
4 ounces semisweet chocolate, chopped

INSTRUCTIONS
1. Put the cream in the pot and put it on the stove. Turn the heat to medium-high and cook until the cream just comes to a boil, 3 to 4 minutes. Keep your eyes on it because you don't want it to overboil.
2. Put the chocolate in the bowl and very, very carefully add the cream, because it can sputter and splatter (this is really a job for an adult).
3. Cover the bowl with the plate and set aside for 5 minutes. Stir until smooth, cover, and refrigerate until it has cooled completely, 45 minutes to 1 hour.
4. Just before serving, put 1 heaping tablespoon of ganache on each cooled cupcake and spread until smooth.

Chocolate Chip Cookies
with Lots of Variations

If you can make great cookies, then you've always got something to bring to a bake sale or potluck—plus, you've got the perfect way to turn a boring Saturday night into a cozy family party.

ADULT NEEDED: YES • HANDS-ON TIME: 20 MINUTES • TOTAL TIME: 35 MINUTES (1 BATCH) • MAKES: 5–6 DOZEN

KITCHEN GEAR
Large mixing bowl
Rubber spatula
Measuring cup
Measuring spoons
Spoon
Baking sheet
Pot holder
Large plate

DID YOU KNOW?

Chocolate chip cookies come in a range of textures, from soft and chewy to thin and crispy, depending on the amounts of each ingredient. For instance, adding more eggs makes a more cakelike texture and replacing more of the flour with ground nuts makes a more crumbly texture.

INGREDIENTS
2   sticks unsalted butter, at room temperature
½   cup white sugar
1   cup light brown sugar
2   large eggs, at room temperature
1   tablespoon vanilla extract
1   cup old-fashioned oats
1   cup all-purpose flour
1   cup whole-wheat flour or whole-wheat graham flour
1   teaspoon baking powder
1   teaspoon baking soda
1   teaspoon kosher salt
2 cups semisweet chocolate chips

INSTRUCTIONS
1. Turn the oven on and set it to 325 degrees.
2. Put the butter, white sugar, and brown sugar in the bowl and mix until smooth and creamy.
3. Add the eggs and vanilla extract and mix well.
4. Scrape down the sides of the bowl with the spatula, add the oats, flour, baking powder, baking soda, and salt and beat until everything is mixed well. Scrape down the sides of the bowl, add the chocolate chips, and mix again. (You can cover and refrigerate the dough up to 1 week.)
5. To form the cookies, break off small pieces of dough, roll them into heaping teaspoon-sized balls, and put them about 2 inches apart on the baking sheet. Using your palm, gently press each ball down to flatten slightly.
6. Carefully put the baking sheet in the oven and bake until the cookies begin to brown at the edges, 12 to 15 minutes. Cool on the baking sheet. Put the cooled cookies on the plate and repeat with the remaining dough.

Be Creative

- **Walnut Chocolate Chip:** Substitute toasted walnuts for half the chocolate chips.
- **Walnut:** Substitute lightly toasted walnuts for all the chocolate chips.
- **White Chocolate–Cranberry:** Substitute a mix of white chocolate chips and dried cranberries for the chocolate chips.
- **Oatmeal Cookies:** Decrease the whole-wheat flour to ½ cup and increase the oats to 2 cups. Take out the baking powder.
- **Cocoa Cookies:** Substitute 1 cup unsweetened cocoa powder for the oats. Decrease the baking powder to ½ teaspoon and take out the chocolate chips.

Molasses Cookies

A little bit spicier than a gingersnap and very adult, but we haven't found a kid yet who doesn't love these. Bet you will, too!

ADULT NEEDED: YES • HANDS-ON TIME: 20 MINUTES • TOTAL TIME: 35 MINUTES (1 BATCH) • MAKES: 3–4 DOZEN

KITCHEN GEAR
Mixing bowl
Rubber spatula
Measuring cup
Measuring spoons
Spoon
Baking sheet
Pot holder
Large plate

Maple Cookies:
Substitute maple syrup for the molasses.

INGREDIENTS
1 ½ sticks unsalted butter, at room temperature
1 cup sugar
1 large egg, at room temperature
¼ cup molasses
1 teaspoon vanilla extract
1 cup all-purpose flour
1 cup whole-wheat flour
2 teaspoons baking soda
1 teaspoon ground cinnamon
½ teaspoon ground ginger
½ teaspoon Kosher salt
½ teaspoon ground cardamom (if you like)

INSTRUCTIONS
1. Turn the oven on and set it to 350 degrees.
2. Put the butter and sugar in the bowl and mix until smooth and creamy.
3. Add the egg, molasses, and vanilla extract and mix well. The mixture will not blend completely and will not be completely smooth. Don't worry.
4. Scrape down the sides of the bowl with the spatula, add the flours, baking soda, cinnamon, ginger, salt, and cardamom (if you like) and stir until everything is mixed in. (You can cover and refrigerate the dough up to 1 week.)
5. To form the cookies: break off small pieces and roll them into 1-inch balls. Put the balls 2 inches apart on the baking sheet. Using your palm, gently press each ball down to flatten slightly.
6. Carefully put the baking sheet in the oven and bake until the cookies begin to brown at the edges, 12 to 15 minutes. Cool on the baking sheet. Put the cooled cookies on the plate and repeat with the remaining dough.

Peanut Butter Cookies

Be sure to read this recipe from start to finish before beginning. There is no flour in it—and that's not a mistake! But trust us, these peanut butter cookies are mostly peanuts and peanut butter, and will be the best, most peanutty peanut butter cookies you'll ever eat.

ADULT NEEDED: YES • HANDS-ON TIME: 20 MINUTES • TOTAL TIME: 35 MINUTES (1 BATCH) • MAKES: 3 DOZEN

KITCHEN GEAR
Baking sheet
Mixing bowl
Rubber spatula
Measuring cup
Measuring spoons
Spoon
Fork
Pot holder
Large plate

Almond Butter Cookies:
Substitute almond butter for the peanut butter and almonds for the peanuts.

INGREDIENTS
2 tablespoons unsalted butter, at room temperature
1 cup creamy or chunky peanut butter, at room temperature
1 cup sugar
1 large egg, at room temperature
1 teaspoon baking soda
½ teaspoon kosher salt
¾ cup roasted peanuts, coarsely chopped

INSTRUCTIONS
1. Turn the oven on and set it to 350 degrees.
2. Put the butter, peanut butter, and sugar in the bowl and mix until smooth and creamy.
3. Add the egg and mix well. Scrape down the sides of the bowl with the spatula, add the baking soda, salt, and peanuts and mix again. The dough will be really crumbly and not seem to come together well. Don't worry.
4. Pinch off pieces of dough and roll them into 1 ½-inch balls. Put them on the prepared baking sheet. Using your clean hand or the bottom of a glass, press each ball down until flattened, and then, using a fork, make a crisscross pattern on top of each cookie.
5. Carefully put the baking sheet in the oven and bake until the cookies are just beginning to brown, about 10 minutes. Set aside to cool for 10 minutes. Put the cooled cookies on a plate, and repeat with remaining dough.

Fruit and Nut Energy Bars

These bars are endlessly adaptable and can be made to fit almost any taste. You can replace some of the nuts with seeds: we especially like pumpkin, sunflower, and sesame. Just be sure to toast them first to bring out their flavor.

ADULT NEEDED: YES (FOR CUTTING AT THE END) • **HANDS-ON TIME: 20 MINUTES** • **TOTAL TIME: 20 MINUTES** • **MAKES: 16 BARS**

KITCHEN GEAR
8 x 8-inch baking pan

Waxed or parchment paper or aluminum foil

Large bowl

Small bowl

Rubber spatula

Sharp knife (adult needed)

INGREDIENTS
½ cup toasted chopped nuts (one kind or a combination of almonds, walnuts, or pecans)

¾ cup dried fruit (one kind or a combination of raisins, currants, dried cranberries, or chopped dates, plums, apricots, or peaches)

¾ cup old-fashioned oats

¾ cup crisp rice cereal

2 tablespoons unsweetened coconut (if you like)

½ cup almond or peanut butter

¼ cup honey, real maple syrup, or agave syrup

½ teaspoon vanilla extract

INSTRUCTIONS
1. Line the pan with waxed or parchment paper or aluminum foil and leave enough hanging over the edges so you can cover the bars later. (You will need a little more than twice as much as the bottom of the pan.)
2. Put the nuts, dried fruit, oats, rice cereal, and coconut, if you like, in the large bowl and toss well.
3. Put the almond butter and honey in the small bowl and microwave until the almond butter is softened, about 30 seconds. Stir until smooth. Add the vanilla extract and stir again until smooth.
4. Pour the almond mixture into the large bowl and mix until well combined.
5. Put the mixture into the prepared pan and pat down as hard as you can. You want to make the bars dense. Using the overhanging waxed paper, cover the bars completely. Cover the pan with plastic wrap and refrigerate at least 4 hours and up to 1 week.
6. Using the knife, cut into 16 bars.

Drinks

It's fun to make your own drinks—and it's a great time to boost the creativity, since it's not difficult and it's not as important as, say, dinner.

But it does matter; keeping your thirst quenched is a good way to make sure you're staying hydrated—and staying hydrated is vital for fitness and good health. If you love to drink plain water, then drink all you can! But if you crave a little flavor, a little something extra, then these recipes are for you.

We start with the flavor and freshness of fruit juices, diluting them with water or sparkling water so they aren't just bombing your body with sugar. Think of them as light, natural soft drinks, and feel free to adapt them with the flavors and ingredients you like best. We've also got a couple of international favorites—a Mexican *agua fresca* and an Indian lassi—as well as a trio of warming drinks perfect for wintry days and, for summery days, a sparkling, fruity ice cube trick. See if you don't develop a thirst for some of these delicious drinks!

Lemon-Honey Sparkle

In some ancient cultures honey used to be so important, it was sometimes used instead of money! Try this sparkling (and valuable) drink—it might remind you of a superlight, fizzy lemonade.

ADULT NEEDED: NO • HANDS-ON TIME: 5 MINUTES • TOTAL TIME: 5 MINUTES • MAKES: 2 SERVINGS

KITCHEN GEAR
Measuring cup
2 tall glasses
Measuring spoons

INGREDIENTS
2 cups sparkling water
2 teaspoons honey
2 teaspoons fresh lemon juice

INSTRUCTIONS
1. Divide the sparkling water between the glasses.
2. Add the honey and lemon juice. Stir well and drink up!

Honey doesn't spoil (if it's in an airtight container). Bacteria are picky about where they live. If the water around the bacteria is too salty, too acidic, or too sweet, then the bacteria can't drink it. In the case of honey, it is both too acidic and too sweet, so the bacteria get dehydrated.

Sealed honey vats found in King Tut's tomb contained honey that was still edible, despite spending more than 2,000 years beneath the sand.

Cucumber-Mint Water

Drinking lots of water is good for you, but sometimes you want it to have a little bit of flavor—that's why we're adding the refreshing combination of cucumber and fresh mint leaves. You can strain the mint and cucumber out of the water before you serve it, but it's not necessary. In fact, sometimes it's nice to get a surprise slice or two of cucumber in your glass. *By Adam Ried*

ADULT NEEDED: YES • HANDS-ON TIME: 5 MINUTES • TOTAL TIME: 15 MINUTES • MAKES: 6 CUPS

KITCHEN GEAR
Vegetable peeler
Sharp knife (adult needed)
Measuring cup
Glass or ceramic pitcher
Wooden spoon

INGREDIENTS
⅓ cup fresh mint leaves
½ cucumber, peeled and thinly sliced
6 cups cold tap water

INSTRUCTIONS
1. Put the mint leaves in the pitcher and using the wooden spoon, gently mash and stir until the leaves look a little crushed.
2. Add the cucumber slices and water, stir, and refrigerate for at least 15 minutes. Serve right away.

Crushing the mint leaves with a wooden spoon is called "muddling," and it helps release their flavor. The spoon breaks open the tiny cells of the mint leaves, causing them to spill out their flavor molecules.

Berry Spritzer

Try this great fizzy, fruity drink. It will satisfy your sweet tooth without filling you up on sugar. *By Adam Ried*

ADULT NEEDED: NO • HANDS-ON TIME: 10 MINUTES • TOTAL TIME: 10 MINUTES • MAKES: 4 SERVINGS

KITCHEN GEAR
Measuring cup
Bowl
Fork or potato masher
4 tall glasses

INGREDIENTS
1 cup berries (any kind is fine), fresh or frozen
4 cups sparkling water
4 lemon or lime slices (if you like)

INSTRUCTIONS
1. Put the berries in the bowl and using your fork or potato masher, break them up until they are mushy.
2. Divide the berry mash among the 4 glasses and top each with 1 cup sparkling water. Add a lemon or lime slice, if you like, and serve right away.

Don't have fresh berries? Frozen are fine! Since berries are usually frozen right after they are picked, they preserve the same nutrients you get from a fresh berry, and sometimes even more. Some nutrients are lost, however, when berries are cooked or canned.

Just as sugar or salt can dissolve in water, gases like carbon dioxide can, too, so you can't see that they are there. In the bottle, the fizzy liquid is under high pressure, which is why a thin plastic bottle can feel rigid. This pressure keeps the carbon dioxide dissolved. However, when you open the bottle, the pressure is released, so not all the carbon dioxide is dissolved. Instead, this extra carbon dioxide forms bubbles that rise to the surface.

Mango Lassi

This sweet-tart treat from India and Pakistan is the perfect way to cool off in the summer heat. It's also a terrific way to cool your mouth in between bites of spicy food.

ADULT NEEDED: YES • HANDS-ON TIME: 10 MINUTES • TOTAL TIME: 10 MINUTES • MAKES: 2 SERVINGS

KITCHEN GEAR:
Blender (adult needed)
Measuring cup
Measuring spoons
2 glasses

INGREDIENTS:
½ cup mango puree or chopped fresh or frozen mango
½ cup plain yogurt
½ cup cold tap water
1 teaspoon fresh lime juice

INSTRUCTIONS
1. Put the mango, yogurt, water, and lime juice in the blender. Put the top on tightly.
2. Turn the blender to medium and blend until the mixture is smooth and frothy.
3. Divide the mixture between the glasses and serve right away, or cover and refrigerate up to 4 hours.

DID YOU KNOW?

Casein, a protein in dairy products, is the reason yogurt and yogurt-based drinks can cool your mouth down when you eat something spicy: it works like a detergent to scrub off the capsaicin, which is the spicy compound in many chiles, and then allows it to be washed away.

Orange-Cranberry Fizz

Hot and tired when you get home from school? Make yourself a refreshing fizzy juice drink, then cool down and relax.

ADULT NEEDED: YES • HANDS-ON TIME: 5 MINUTES • TOTAL TIME: 5 MINUTES • MAKES: 4 SERVINGS

KITCHEN GEAR
Cutting board
Sharp knife (adult needed)
Measuring cup
Pitcher
Mixing spoon
4 tall glasses

INGREDIENTS
3 cups sparkling water
½ cup orange juice (if you're using a fresh orange, grate in a bit of the zest, too, for added flavor!)
½ cup unsweetened cranberry juice
1 lime, cut into quarters

INSTRUCTIONS
1. Put the sparkling water in the pitcher, add the orange and cranberry juices, and stir well.
2. Divide the mixture among the glasses and add 1 lime wedge to each. Serve right away.

Be Creative
You can use almost any kind of real juice instead of the orange and cranberry. Great combinations include orange/grapefruit, grapefruit/cranberry, and apple/cranberry.

Watermelon Agua Fresca

This is a popular drink in Mexico and some other Latin American countries. The words *agua fresca* mean "fresh water" in Spanish, and there are lots of popular flavors—but this is one of the easiest, and tastiest, to make at home.
By Adam Ried

ADULT NEEDED: YES • HANDS-ON TIME: 10 MINUTES • TOTAL TIME: 1 HOUR AND 10 MINUTES • MAKES: 4 CUPS

KITCHEN GEAR
Cutting board
Sharp knife (adult needed)
Measuring cup
Measuring spoons
Food processor or blender (adult needed)
Small spoon

INGREDIENTS
2 ¼ pounds cold seedless watermelon
1 cup very cold tap water
1 tablespoon fresh lime juice
A pinch kosher salt
1 ½ tablespoons honey (if you like)

INSTRUCTIONS
1. Cut the watermelon flesh away from the rind (this is a job for an adult). Cut the watermelon into chunks.
2. Put the watermelon chunks, water, lime juice, salt, and honey, if you like, in the food processor or blender. Put the top on tightly.
3. Turn the food processor or blender to medium and blend until the mixture is liquidy and smooth.
4. Serve right away, or cover and refrigerate up to 4 hours. Stir before serving.

What is composting?

It's when you save and reuse food waste (like banana peels, watermelon rinds, and coffee grounds) by letting it decompose outside to create a very rich soil for the plants in your garden.

Fun, Fruity Ice Cubes

Freezing fruit into ice cubes is super easy, and it's a great way to dress up a glass of plain or sparkling water. The fruit in the cubes looks pretty and tastes great, too.

Simply drop a berry or small piece of fruit into each compartment of an ice cube tray, then fill with cold tap water and freeze until solid, around 3 hours. Use any fruit (or fresh herbs) that appeal to you. Have an adult help you with cutting up the fruit, and make sure the pieces are small enough to fit into the compartments. *By Adam Ried*

Try some of these yummy additions:

WHOLE
grapes
raspberries
blackberries
blueberries
cherries
mint or basil leaves

SLICED
strawberries
oranges
lemons
limes

DICED
mangoes
kiwi
pineapple
peach

DID YOU KNOW?

Raspberries and blackberries are made up of clusters of little beadlike juice sacs, called "drupelets," which are arranged around a central core.

Warm Mulled Cider

"Mulled" means heating up liquid with ingredients like cinnamon sticks that will gently flavor it. Mulled cider tastes like liquid apple pie! *By Adam Ried*

ADULT NEEDED: YES • HANDS-ON TIME: 5 MINUTES • TOTAL TIME: 40 MINUTES • MAKES: 1 QUART

KITCHEN GEAR
Vegetable peeler
Medium-sized pot
Measuring cup
Slotted spoon
4 mugs or cups
Pot holder

INGREDIENTS
1 orange, scrubbed
2 cinnamon sticks
4 cups apple cider

INSTRUCTIONS
1. Using the vegetable peeler, remove long strips of zest (the orange part, not the white part underneath) from half of the orange.
2. Put the cinnamon sticks, orange zest, and cider in the pot and put it on the stove. Turn the heat to medium-high and heat until the cider is steaming—about 7 minutes. Turn the heat down to low and cook for 30 minutes.
3. Carefully, using the slotted spoon, remove the orange zest and cinnamon sticks and throw them away.
4. Divide the cider among the mugs and serve right away.

Hot Honey-Vanilla Milk

Surely you've had chocolate milk and cocoa. Now how about trying something a little different?

ADULT NEEDED: YES • HANDS-ON TIME: 10 MINUTES • TOTAL TIME: 10 MINUTES • MAKES: 2 SERVINGS

KITCHEN GEAR
Measuring cup
Measuring spoons
Small pot
Whisk or spoon
2 mugs or cups
Pot holder

INGREDIENTS
2 cups low-fat or whole milk, soy milk, or rice milk
2 teaspoons honey or real maple syrup
½ teaspoon vanilla extract
A pinch ground cinnamon

INSTRUCTIONS
1. Put all the ingredients in the pot and put it on the stove. Turn the heat to medium-low and cook until warm, about 3 minutes.
2. Whisk or stir the milk from time to time.
3. Carefully divide the warm milk between the mugs and serve right away.

DID YOU KNOW?

You might know a lot of passionate chocolate lovers (we do, too!), but **vanilla extract is actually the most popular flavor in the entire world!** Vanilla extract is steeped from vanilla beans, which grow from vanilla flowers, a type of orchid. The flowers can only be pollinated by one particular mountain bee, native to Mexico: the bee buzzes so crazily that it breaks through the flower, spreading pollen from stamen to pistil. The pollinated orchid then swells into a podlike fruit that you might have seen: a vanilla bean.

Hot Cocoa, Mexican Style

This very rich and satisfying winter drink is probably not as sweet as what you're used to: our version is all about the chocolate flavor and warming spices, traditional to the drink made and served in Mexico.

ADULT NEEDED: YES • HANDS-ON TIME: 10 MINUTES • TOTAL TIME: 10 MINUTES • MAKES: 2 SERVINGS

KITCHEN GEAR
Small pot

Measuring cup

Measuring spoons

Fork or whisk

2 mugs or cups

INGREDIENTS
1 ½ cups low-fat or whole milk

1 ½ tablespoons unsweetened cocoa powder

2 ½ teaspoons honey or sugar

¾ teaspoon vanilla extract

¾–1 teaspoon ground cinnamon

A pinch chili powder, if you like it spicy

INSTRUCTIONS
1. Put the milk in the pot. Put the pot on the stove and turn the heat to low.
2. Heat the milk until it is very warm, about 3 minutes. Be sure to keep your eye on it; you don't want it to boil or burn.
3. Turn the heat off and add the cocoa powder, honey, vanilla extract, cinnamon, and the chili powder, if you like it spicy. Using the whisk, whip the milk until the top is frothy.
4. Divide the cocoa between the mugs and serve right away.

What is the origin of cocoa? Chocolate starts out as seeds from the cacao tree, which are too bitter to eat. The word "cacao" probably came from the Olmec (the first Mexican civilization) word *kakawa*, more than 3,000 years ago. For hundreds of years, the Aztecs, Mayans, and other Central and South Americans used cacao beans in a spicy beverage, with flavorings like vanilla, chile, herbs, and flowers. In the sixteenth and seventeenth centuries, Europeans added milk and sugar to the drink, making it resemble the hot chocolate of today.

Acknowledgments

There are so, so many people to thank: this cookbook was inspired by *ChopChop: The Fun Cooking Magazine for Families*, and *ChopChop* is really, more than anything I have ever worked on, a team effort.

First and foremost there would be no magazine without Steven Slon, Andrzej Janerka, Carl Tremblay, Mary Jo Viederman, and Kerry Michaels, all of whom signed on when *ChopChop* was little more than an idea. They took my rambling thoughts and worked tirelessly to turn the magazine into the beauty it is today. Similarly, Dr. Barry Zuckerman, Dr. Lisa Simpson, Sue Denny, Hana Nobel, Ann Marchetti, Andrew Steinberg, David Cutler, Dr. David Ludwig, Dr. Walter Willett, Fiona Wilson, and John Willoughby lent their smarts when there was little evidence of success. Also, thanks go to Christine Madigan, Peter Nirenberg, Jill Ryan, Dr. Shale Wong, Dr. Jose Alberto Betances, Mollie Katzen, Vivien Morris, Tina Peel, Jane Pemberton, Dr. Ellen Rome, William C. Taylor, Helen Veit, Christina D. Economos, Dr. Christopher Duggan, Dr. Shirley Huang, Cathy Chute, Sharon Sprague, Katie Henry, Pam Banks, Mary Jane Sawyer, Megan Bloch, Molly Santry, and Noreen Bigelow.

Huge thanks go to all the families who lent us their kitchens—and, more importantly, to those who lent us their gorgeous, funny, smart, curious children. Special thanks to Urit Chaimovitz and Jon Bloch, who opened their home to us over and over again (despite several mishaps). Most importantly, thanks to the New Balance Foundation, which has supported *ChopChop* in all ways possible, and to the American Academy of Pediatrics, who shouted our praises from the mountaintops.

Catherine Newman is *ChopChop*'s editor, and not only does she contribute everything important to the magazine, both her eye and her palate are on every single page of this cookbook: I literally could not have done it without her. Gina Hahn is our tireless and wonderful copy editor; she ensures that everything makes sense. Adam Ried contributed lots of humor and beverage recipes, and Naveen Sinha explained every possible scientific aspect of every recipe.

Carl Tremblay's photographs are, as usual, stunning, and all the more so with the help of ace assistant Ryan Hickey and stylist Catrine Kelty. Vic DeRobertis took the whole mess and turned it into the beautiful cookbook you are now holding. Everyone at Simon & Schuster, especially Sammy Perlmutter, who pursued us, has been great: Michael Szczerban, Carly Sommerstein, Faren Bachelis, Jonathan Evans, Nancy Singer, Lewelin Polanco, Larry Pekarek, Leah Johanson, Marie Kent, and Jackie Seow, among them.

And nothing would ever happen without my wonderful agent, Carla Glasser, and her longtime accomplice, Jenny Alperen, who are, as always, fun, funny, and invaluable.

Index

About ChopChop
and Sally Sampson

ChopChopKids, the publisher of *ChopChop: The Fun Cooking Magazine for Families*, is an innovative nonprofit organization whose mission is to inspire and teach kids to cook real food with their families. We believe that cooking and eating together as a family is a vital step in resolving the obesity and hunger epidemics and will create a needed cultural transformation.

Endorsed by the American Academy of Pediatrics, *ChopChop* is a quarterly magazine named the 2013 Publication of the Year by the James Beard Foundation and winner of the 2013 Parents Choice Magazine Award (gold). *ChopChop* is available in English and Spanish and reaches over two million families annually. The magazine is available in every state in the United States and in seven other countries.

ChopChop was named a USDA Strategic Partner and a media partner of Partnership for a Healthier America. It can be found in nearly half of American pediatrician offices and in stores and community centers around the country.

For more information on subscribing to *ChopChop*, visit www.chopchopmag.org.

Sally Sampson is the founder of ChopChopKids and the author and coauthor of numerous cookbooks, including *The $50 Dinner Party*, *Throw Me a Bone* (with Cooper Gillespie), and *The Olives Table* (with Todd English). She has contributed to *Self*, *Bon Appétit*, *Food & Wine*, *The Atlantic*, the *Boston Globe*, and the *Boston Phoenix*. She lives in Watertown, Massachusetts.